GROWING ADULTS ON SUNDAY MORNING

KNUTE LARSON

VICTOR BOOKS®

A DIVISION OF SCRIPTURE PRESS PUBLICATIONS INC.
USA CANADA ENGLAND

Copyediting: Afton B. Rorvik
Cover Design: Joe DeLeon
Cover Photo/Illustration: Ted Wright
Interior Illustrations: Don Jeffrey

Library of Congress Cataloging-in-Publication Data

Larson, Knute.
    Growing adults on Sunday morning / Knute Larson.
      p.   cm.
    Includes bibliographical references.
    ISBN 0-89693-822-0
    1. Christian education of adults. 2 Sunday schools. I. Title.
  BV1488.L37 1991
  268'.434—dc20   91-24336
                                                  CIP

1 2 3 4 5 6 7 8 9 10 Printing/Year 95 94 93 92 91

GROWING ADULTS ON SUNDAY MORNING

CONTENTS

DEDICATION

To my father, Robert "Pete" Larson,
whose death, while I was reading galley
proofs for this book, reminded me
of the delight of good adult friendship
and encouragement.
I will miss his applause
and love.

And to his church, Melrose Gardens Grace Brethren
Church in Harrisburg, Pa., who
carried out so many of the concepts
of this book for Dad in his senior years
just as it did for me in the crucial
pre-teen and teen years.
I am grateful.

ONE

The Need for ABFs

"Pastor, I understand your concerns, but the Sunday School is really my area. You take care of the church, and I will take care of the Sunday School."

A Sunday School superintendent in western Pennsylvania was talking with his pastor, and it was tense. Very.

They had a separate Sunday School constitution. And they had a separate Sunday School offering. The Sunday School had its own "opening exercises." A short worship service. Often the superintendent gave a brief devotional or sermonette. They took a birthday offering. Latecomers straggled in.

The pastor sat frustrated.

The tense discussion was over possible changes in the Sunday School arrangement. The superintendent was all for going back to tradition, something like the separation of church and state, the cleavage between church and Sunday School. The pastor had some new ideas.

On another day, in another state, another pastor is also upset.

"I get so frustrated with all the lists of people that I have,"

Pastor Mooreland says to his secretary. "I have a list of newcomers, a list of members, a list for each Adult Sunday School class, a list for our Thursday night evangelism, and a care list from the deacons. I need a list of all the lists that we have." His smile was one of helplessness.

The concept and organization of Adult Bible Fellowship arose from dilemmas like these.

What Are Adult Bible Fellowships?
Some people like to call them Sunday Schools. All right. But they are more.

They are what they say they are.

Adult: They are for college age and up, to meet their special needs.

Bible: They major on the teaching and application of the Word of God to daily living.

Fellowship: They also major on relationships and caring love, a huge need in our world.

Adult Bible Fellowships are groups for study and fellowship, organized around the Sunday morning adult Bible study hour, often called Sunday School.

They have guidelines and goals, and much variety.

The Reasons for ABFs:

1. *Fellowship.* Adults can get Bible teaching from sermons, tapes, the radio, home Bible studies, and Sunday School. Yet in surveys all over the country about why adults come to Sunday School, the number one reason is fellowship. Relationships. Getting to know others.

ABFs are organized on Sundays and throughout the week—to provide that fellowship. The Sunday session time is built around it and so is the Bible study. The responsibilities of the class leaders are built around fellowship too.

2. *Bible.* As with most adult Sunday groupings, or other Bible

studies, the Bible is featured. ABFs challenge adults to study God's Word and apply it.

It's one thing to believe in the authority or inerrancy of the Bible, but to see its personal application and want to do something about it is a different matter altogether. ABFs promote that.

3. *Outreach.* A church of any size needs outreach. The ABFs include a plan to bring those on the "fringe" of the church or those outside the church into these smaller groups.

4. *Pastoral Care.* In any group over 70 or 80, people will get missed. Studies show us that when a church reaches that size, people easily drop out or conclude that they do not fit in with the main group.

One pastor can't do it all. ABFs include a whole system of caring and hospital visitation and meeting of special needs. No one will be left out.

5. *Ministry.* ABFs involve many more people in ministry than the average adult Sunday School. And it is not just busy work. It is fulfillment of the commands of the Bible related to caring about people.

In a rushing world, in growing churches, for people feeling like a number, ABFs stand tall. They can really help. Adult Bible Fellowships are a way to organize adults in a church into groups of growing and loving relationships. A way of combining many lists into one.

They work.

The Need for Manageable Units
It all started when, as a pastor of an ambitious church, I realized how many lists I had and how much guilt I felt about the commands in the Bible for me to "one another" these people. To exhort them, to encourage them, to get them to do that to one another, to warn them, to build them, to get them doing that to one another.

But we were spread in so many directions. They met in one group for Sunday School, another group for prayer meeting, and another group for home Bible study.

We were in one worship service and then two and then three.

We could say "Hello" and "How are you?" but not a whole lot more. That can be superficial. Someone could miss three weeks or five in a row and nobody would know it.

What to do?

Adult Bible Fellowships were the answer, combining Bible study, care, social relationships, and evangelism into one ministering unit within the local church. They are the "congregation" that Peter Wagner calls for when he lists the experiences of the church in *Your Church Can Be Healthy* (Abingdon Press, p. 23):

CELEBRATION—Looking up, in worship, and to the Word, for motivation.

CONGREGATION—Groups within the church where you know each other and where someone is missed when he is not there. They are organized for fellowship, study and growth, and outreach.

CELLS—Small groups from 7–12, where there is growing intimacy and discipleship.

CORE—The home—taught and encouraged at church.

The middle-sized group is clearly needed. While some church

analysts—just a few—argue that only "celebration" and "cell" are needed in a church, something is missing when there is not good congregational life. These leaders are thinking the Korean model should be duplicated in our culture.

Congregation was, after all, one of the main purposes of the early church as depicted in Acts 2:42-46. Those people were meeting together a lot, helping each other, standing in awe and worship, sharing, and finding favor with the outsiders.

I'm not going to call these groups ABFs, but I am going to say that this again is an argument for having some kind of smaller groups within the church where this can happen. Certainly as the church grew to thousands, they did not do all these things together. But believers met in smaller groups and they got to know each other and people could tell that they loved each other.

The church that wants to stay at a maximum of 70 to 90 adults can get by with one congregation, made up of the people that go to the celebration service.

But the church that wants to grow beyond these numbers must choose to have various congregations with the church. And I believe these groups are best managed and facilitated by meeting together on Sunday morning. I also believe that people fellowship best with affinity groups—people nearly their same age and with similar interests.

If a church just does the large group and then the small cell groups, using the model of Cho's church in Seoul, Korea, it misses the whole web of relationships that happen when a larger group exists.

Recently, I attended one of the largest churches in America and sat down with some of their staff, all of whom shared a wonderful and positive spirit about Christ and their church. But several mentioned that there's something missing in their church and they are trying to find it.

They were very strong on home groups. And the worship or celebration service, helped by having one of the finest speakers in the country, was excellent.

But most members were mixing with only five or six couples in their home groups, and they wanted to get something going that would help them get to know others at the church.

You just can't do that at celebration.

Even the medium-sized church can benefit from trying to multiply congregations. Congregational life is 20 to 70 or 80 or 90 people getting to know and trust each other and studying the Bible in that context of fellowship and love. That we call an Adult Bible Fellowship.

About sixteen years ago, I got so frustrated pastoring a church of five or six hundred. I had lists for Thursday evening visitation, membership lists, deacons' lists, Sunday School class lists, and a couple of others. And we didn't have computers then. I was the only pastor trying to correlate it all. How in the world could we get all this together?

We broke the whole church into Adult Bible Fellowships. Didn't vote on it. Didn't tell anybody. I began teaching a young adult class and tried to form what was, in my mind, the first Adult Bible Fellowship in the world. I wanted this to be more than an old-time Sunday School class.

I remember the first year I said, carefully, "We're not going to vote on a president this year. We're going to have a class leader and I'll appoint him." I didn't say it that directly, but that's what happened. Les had been the president three years in a row. The most popular guy. But he wasn't good at doing anything behind the scenes. He just liked to be up front. So I appointed a class leader.

What Is an ABF?

It is a group or community of people committed to know and apply the Word together in a caring fellowship, with organization to bring about pastoral care, discipleship and outreach—usually divided by age groupings so there is natural affinity and strong bonding.

Then we asked somebody else to be in charge of caring systems, and our deacons' list was thrown into the ABF. Our outreach list was also included, so that everything was organized under my working as the adult director in the church with a teacher, a class leader, whom I appointed for his heart, and a care captain. These all served with me as a committee to produce true congregational life—a community of believers within the church.

At first nobody thought it was anything different, but gradually the class began growing. Later we split up. And then we used those two ABFs as a model for the rest of the Bible Fellowships. Soon we had six and then eight and then nine and ten. Now I am in a church with over thirty ABFs.

The Need to Reach Adults

Who is it we are trying to reach through the church? Certainly the children. Certainly the youth. But just as surely, the adults.

Often the education priorities of the church are illustrated by the hiring of the "second man." The youth pastor. A lot of church leaders feel that if there's a good program for children, the parents will come. I have heard it 100 times: "If you have a good youth program, you win the whole family."

That is not always true. Many adults are not parents! And many others are single parents who need special opportunities for friendship and support.

The beauty of Adult Bible Fellowships is that they deal with the real issue that parents and other adults and singles feel so strongly—the need for fellowship and study.

People often think that if a church generates programs for children and has something really alive for youth, that settles program questions. Not so. Not so.

Adults want their joy too! They want fellowship and an atmosphere of warmth and learning. Adults crave meaningful relationships as much as youth, perhaps more, in that they can define it better!

It's not so much the rising interest in adult education that says this is the time for ABFs, though there certainly is a trend that way. Even more significant is the rising awareness of relationship needs. People are admitting that vacuum more than

15

ever before, especially younger adults, who have grown up claiming candor as their middle name.

Adult Bible Fellowships are a church's attempt to get to the hearts of adults and help them touch each other as well as the Word. And when that happens, adults come. And they usually bring their children and youth.

Some say that the main bridges that connect the church with young adults, especially those labeled Baby Boomers, are worship and vision. They love to sing in worship, or feel like a service really honors God. They respond to visionary leadership that gives a sense of direction.

But there is a third bridge: relationships. Not "Hi, how are you?" relationships, but true and growing friendships built on openness and love.

The young adult will go to an ABF for the exposure and link to people who stand with him in the battles of life. He will not thrive on the Bible content as much as on the touches and encouragement from people nearly his age.

This bridge is best built by a well-planned ABF system.

The Need to Emphasize Relationships

When we talk ABFs, we are not talking curriculum. It is related, but not the key issue. Study what you like.

When we talk ABFs, we are not talking a way of study either. We always advocate student involvement of course. Many publishers spent time in the '70s and early '80s seeking to teach adult teachers how to teach. To get the class involved. To help people see and feel and discuss and not just listen. I think they brought good ideas.

But Adult Bible Fellowships are about pastoring and caring and sharing and fellowship. They attempt to do in a manageable group what the Bible seems to tell the church to do.

That must be why I am so excited about them!

I've seen people who started in the church as spectators, sitting in the balcony or pretty far back on the main floor, try an ABF through a friend, and get hooked on the beauty of fellowship.

I've seen couples who live far away, drive to the anonymity of a large church and experience joy in the worship service but also get to know new friends and really enjoy each other in the ABF "congregation."

In every survey I have ever seen about why adults go to Sunday School, the number one reason is fellowship. We could wish they would have said that they wanted to be trained for service or motivated to minister to each other. Those may become aftermaths and related benefits. But the number one reason that people attend a smaller group in a church, according to surveys I have seen and every couple I have asked, is fellowship.

Friends. Caring partners.

In a world where people are treated as numbers, in a place where loneliness is prevalent no matter how big the crowd or active the schedule, in a world where even Christians do not do too well listening when they ask, "How are you?" Adult Bible Fellowships are important.

The Need for Bible Study
Of course the need for good Bible study is behind all of this. But the best Bible study, over the long haul, happens in a setting where you are with people you are getting to know and love.

You are more open to God's truth in such a setting, and candid questions or application suggestions come much easier.

Bible study in a group can happen very effectively in an ABF. (Other chapters will elaborate on this.)

Today some church specialists are putting enticing subtitles on kits and books about the Sunday School, celebrating this way of outreach, care, and fellowship as if it is a brand new toy!

It has been around for a long time, but Sunday School has often been treated as a necessary good thing, but rather vanilla.

No, No!

TWO

Becoming a Stronger Church

I grew up in a church where members annually made a commitment called a rededication. For me as a young teenager it sort of meant, I'm going to do better this year.

I've said that about my marriage to Jeanine. We've said after a tough time or maybe an inspiring moment, "We're going to make this better." But what happens when you do that is a bit of guilt, a bit of adrenalin, and usually the same old story.

I made a specific decision about marriage when my wife hit me on the head with a four by eight (not a two by four) about our third year in a church and said, "I think you're doing a great job with the church, but I don't think I know you." I swallowed like you do when you're not sure what to say next and I thought, *Well, I have a choice here between building a strong church and losing my wife at the same time or changing some things in my schedule.* She didn't have her suitcase packed, she just obviously had an emotional separation that I wasn't as aware of as she was. That often happens to men. We started at that time, now over twenty years ago, going out to breakfast every Thursday as a symbol of our need to save time for each other each day and every week.

That helped. That was so much better than just, "Come on, let's do better."

Rather than ask churches simply to rededicate themselves, this chapter talks about specific ways to analyze church life so that weaknesses can be pinpointed and corrected. The big question we have to answer is: What kind of experience should people have when they're at the church?

Celebration, or Worship

First, we need to experience celebration.

Celebration is when you look up to God and receive His Word. It is Easter every week. A celebration service can grow to somewhere around 900,000, after which it's good to break into branch churches or maybe split up into smaller groups.

I sat in Cleveland Stadium once with Billy Graham and 87,000 people, and nobody there said, "Oh my, we don't all know each other," or "This place is getting too big." (Now when I said I was with Billy Graham, I mean he was down in the infield and I was up in right field.) 87,000 of us sang "How Great Thou Art!" It was a fabulous celebration.

If your church is over 150, you are too big for everybody to know everybody. But that is not the purpose of the celebration service. Whether you have 30 people or 300 or 3,000, you're not there to hold hands. Celebration is to look up to God and to hear His Word and to celebrate who He is.

When you analyze the celebration of your church, ask yourself: Does it have the spirit of Easter? Does it have joy?

It needs to be done with excellence. I have been in a church where the leader might say in the middle of the service, "Ed, I wonder if you could help with the offering and, Tom, could you help?" As a young person I didn't care, but I didn't bring my friends either because the place wasn't well organized, even though it was celebration.

In your celebration, is there a spirit that Christ is alive? I ask myself, Am I ready for it? Do I make this, as pastor, my major call of the week? Have I got something to say? It doesn't matter

19

about other emergencies. This is an emergency—I've got to do my best in the pulpit every week. And brother, I know on Saturday afternoon at 3 o'clock if I'm still waiting for that sermon to grip my heart and make me cry or laugh, I'm in trouble. Or rather, the congregation is in trouble; or rather, we're all in trouble. And that happens.

Celebration and worship are a wave in this country. Worship has become not just the property of certain brands of Christianity but a passion for many. We want to learn how to worship God.

It's not just the sermon and the singing, but they are a big part of it. Celebration includes prayer and responses and quiet and offerings.

It's fine that people sit in rows for this and that the leaders treat the people gathered as a large group. In fact, if this group is treated as a small gathering, it will stay that way.

Celebration needs to be alive with enthusiasm and sincerity flowing from the leaders' hearts.

When possible, I believe celebration is best when unified and thematic so that people walk out with one main idea and challenge rather than a shotgun blast of twenty ideas.

At this gathering we preach relationships and model them with personal illustrations, but we aren't actively fellowshipping. We come to the celebration experience to worship and celebrate our Lord, to hear from Him, to be motivated toward His grace.

A growing number of books have been written about celebration life in the church. My purpose here is simply to say celebration should be treated differently than the second type of experience if adults are to be reached effectively.

Congregation, or Community

The second kind of experience we want people to have in the church is so important and often missed—congregation, or community. We have about thirty "congregations" or communities within our church, most called Adult Bible Fellowships. I believe they meet true adult needs with a true biblical format.

Congregations are groups within a church formed for mutual encouragement, pastoral care and even outreach. Within this context of love and warmth, members study the Bible.

They are what a church is meant to be.

The best size for a congregation is between 20 and 70 or 90. Any group that gets above 70 or 90 is too big for people to know each other. When a church gets over 70 or 80 adults you can no longer really relate to each other. It gets so big that something happens in the chemistry.

Here's another sociological fact: One man can pastor about 90 people. That's why the main leveling off of the church is about 110, possibly 70 or 80 adults and 20 or 30 children. Often one pastor is doing it all.

In many cases, a church has one adult class that's now 70 adults, and it's hard to grow. People come and they don't feel welcome. Why? The class members have all the friends they can handle. I'm saying churches have got to break down their larger church. The big celebration can go to 900,000 or whatever number the church chooses! But then we must break it down into congregations or communities of people who relate to each other and who see each other every Sunday.

Congregations promote friendships, mutual ministries, and joy. They are organized for fellowship, caring, and fun. They are a wonderful place for the Word of God to be taught, with strong emphasis on accountability. Electives can kill this idea of people getting to know each other because people only meet together for ten or thirteen weeks. Any church that wants to grow and levels off at the common plateau of either 110 or 230 or so, probably needs to have more adoption units, more congregations. If your church does not have more than one or two congregations for people to choose from, you're missing something.

Churches over 130 or 150 in today's culture need to be organized by age, or at least the approximate age of your children. Young marrieds at least need to meet by themselves because they are so into dealing with their needs. It is natural that your five best friends are within a few years of your age. Most people find their close friends and their fellowship affinity with people who have children approximately the age of their own children.

I think the church misses it sometimes when we have people

so scattered and going here and there on Sunday and changing electives every few months and never getting quality fellowship.

You almost have to meet together like this on Sundays. That's when the natives go to church. If you push me on this and say that we're just talking about an old adult Sunday School class, I would say old Sunday School classes as I knew them were a teacher and a class, with lots of content. People don't need content. They have all the content they want. They can watch and listen to tapes, read books, and study. They need fellowship, which you cannot get on tape or alone. ABFs still have teaching, 35-40 minutes, but they get people involved. They provide the fellowship people crave. If one man can pastor 90 people, and if people can have 70 or 90 friends or acquaintances, and if the barriers of a group go up after a certain size, then we definitely need congregations. It is the setting where the "one another" commands of God's Word will be fulfilled.

Look at your church. Are there multiple congregations so people can choose where to serve and grow? Are they organized for caring and fellowship, joy and outreach?

Cells, or Small Groups

The third experience needed in the church's ministry to adults is Cell.

Here seven to twelve is the size, with many saying nine is the best number. (When you have twelve you know one of them is a traitor!) If you have only two people, it's not really a group or a cell. These are breakfast groups, Bible study groups, discipleship or accountability teams. You want a small group where you can be really candid.

The church needs to provide these experiences for adults. Many cells today are built around discipleship and Bible study, but some are also support groups.

We have one cell of former felons. We have a group for alcoholics that meets at the church. We also have support groups for adult children of alcoholics, single parents, college students, and other people with similar special needs or goals.

Robert Schuller often says in his seminars for pastors, "Find a need and meet it. Find a hurt and heal it." If you're in Kansas, I think you'd have a support group for farmers and probably meet at 5 A.M. or Saturdays in the afternoon or something. It's different everywhere. I led one Bible study cell early Wednesday mornings for nine CEOs or managers who lead people and who met for support because theirs is a lonely job. They studied the Bible together, swapped stories and applications, and held each other accountable.

I understand it is best when you first get people involved to have a terminal time—four weeks and then they're done. Often the decision to go longer comes after the good initial experience.

Cells are where you can get accountability.

In the celebration services, you breed conviction or motivation with the Bible content. When people walk out of our church on Sunday morning after a sermon and celebration on the name of Jesus, I hope they know how holy that name is and that their lives can be lived under its banner. I pray that they will want to do that! I don't care if they didn't memorize four verses and they didn't meet a lot of people. I really don't. I want them to go away with conviction and motivation and the experience of worship-celebration.

In the congregations, content with application is a big thing—and fellowship. You can ask questions. You hear others tell what the scriptural principles say to them. You are not in a hurry. You are with friends, and there is an atmosphere of love.

In cell you add other ingredients—accountability and transparency. If I have been meeting with nine men over a long term, I have a few of them I can be very transparent with. I'm going to do it there, but not so much in a group of sixty people.

In your church are there cells to choose from, in and out of the congregations?

Core, or Family

Another essential experience or framework is the core, and it is the family. When we analyze the church here all we can do is decide, are we teaching and modeling and supporting this area enough? Are we giving people incentive and talking to them? Do we have groups that really help?

Colleague or Counseling

A fifth area in which the church should be helping adults is the multi-faceted area of encouraging friendship counseling, one-on-one discipleship, triads of friends who meet for mutual support, or pastoral counseling.

Analyze your church in these five areas. I can rate the church I am a part of from one to ten on every one of those. Not perfectly objectively, I'm sure, but I know where we are weak. And I know where we are strong. You know about yours.

Adult Ministries in the Church
(and how they fit with ABFs if they do)

Celebration services (Worship services that help people look up to God and hear from His Word and worship Him).

These are the main Sunday services usually, and they become the pool from which you draw for the participants in the adult fellowships. ABFs should frequently be mentioned at the celebration services.

They should not be treated as an ABF or a one congregation, or they will stay that way and be limited in size to 90 or less.

The mood conveyed here will support ABFs and urge people to get involved in ABFs and in honesty and the good things that can happen in smaller groups in the church.

Congregations or communities

These are the ABFs and other groups. Choir can be this if it has a caring system and social and outreach life.

Cell groups

A. *Bible studies*

ABFs can support large Bible studies, but they should also have a number where content and application happen in a small group setting where discussion and questions are important.

Most ABFs of 60 or 70 adults can support at least two or three Bible studies that meet in various areas, perhaps by geography of the people in the class. They certainly

---

should be promoted in the ABF, with recognition that not everybody will want to be a part of one.

B. *Discipleship groups*

Certain discipleship groups have a specific goal of training participants for ministry in certain areas, others simply encourage growth from a certain point. Usually someone is the leader, a discipler, and there is a sense of accountability.

ABFs ought to have several of these groups so members have choices, and they should be limited to five to eight people. Normally the best setting for discipleship is an all male group or an all female group, with seven or eight involved.

An ABF of about 60 or 70 adults can certainly support four or five of these groups.

C. *Special need support groups*

While these groups might meet specific needs that relate to many within the entire church, particular ABFs might have special needs. For instance, an ABF that ministers to people in their 40s might have a support group for people resolving differences or hostilities with their parents for that is often the time for adults to bond with their parents.

Support groups for young mothers and a whole program for mothers' clubs can be very effective for the younger ABFs of course. Sometimes within the young married ABFs it is healthy to have a support group just for young mothers.

Young adults also could quietly sponsor a support group for eating disorders or other special needs that might plague that age.

D. *Ministry teams*

Each ABF could consider having a ministry team for particular departmental teaching at the church or a ministry team for music or evangelism. Sometimes the best relationships and discipleship happens between people when they are planning ministry and helping each other gear up for it and do it effectively.

Core (The Family)

Many training and motivating ministries at the church can support the families at home.

A. *Support Groups*

There are many wonderful books and study materials for new parents, or parents of preschoolers or adolescents. Just meeting to pray for each other and then discussing a chapter of a book can be good.

B. *Training Electives*

Classes designed to teach parents and promote interaction can be scheduled on the church calendar frequently. The bigger the church, the more frequent these should be.

C. *Retreats*

We model our Marriage Enjoyment Weekends after the very successful Marriage Encounter Retreats of the Catholic church, but any format that promotes candid evaluation and discussion between couples can be very healthy.

Colleague (or Counseling)

Each church can provide motivation for friendships and opportunities for one-on-one counseling, formal and informal. Triads of men or women can be promoted and encouraged to meet for 10 weeks or so for mutual support.

ABFs Strengthen the Church

My plea is that we do more than just say, "We must become a better church!" There are specific ways to improve—manageable areas in which to begin.

I believe strongly that adults need opportunities to participate in these five basic experiences within a church, and that the Adult Bible Fellowship format provides the best kind of congregational life possible.

Most people have to choose. If you said to me, "People will take only two of those experiences, which two would you rather they take?" I would stutter a little. It depends on the person. Our own church has some who come to congregation and cell and never come to celebration. (I'm sure they buy my sermon tapes.) But that's their choice. I wish they would come. That is part ego, but I also know that the mood of the church is set in celebration services. That's where I do most of my pastoring in terms of content.

Some people come to celebration but skip congregation and cell. Others have celebration and congregation experiences regularly.

I was standing in the hallway greeting some visitors before the third service one Sunday morning. A couple came in from one of the largest churches in America, one of the fastest growing, where they are part of a Sunday morning crowd of thousands. They asked me how our church works.

I could say it in a few seconds or a few hours — but I gave them the shorter answer. I mentioned celebration in the worship service. I spoke of congregational life, within the ABFs, and invited them to attend one so they would get to know other people and get some names on their first visit. And then I told them about some home groups or cells, which would not be meeting that day.

I disagree with church growth people who teach that the church needs to offer only the large celebration and the small cell. Often they have based their teaching on the Cho model in Korea — a different culture, and a church that could use some "congregational life," as ABFs cause it!

One of the best of church analysts, Carl George, likes to picture the church as "something that looks like a large dinosaur, only get up close and you find out it's a lot of little mice." In other words, the church looks like a big place, but you get up close and find all these cell groups — study groups or care groups or discipleship groups or home groups. George teaches that "Mega-church life revolves around two events: the meeting of small groups, or cells; and corporate worship, or celebration" (*Christianity Today,* June 24, 1991, p. 46).

Fine.

The smaller gathering, cell, offers a lot of things we need. But I believe Christians without congregational life are missing something essential whether in a huge mega-church or in a smaller church with only two or three congregations or "communities."

Advantages of ABFs

A manageable system is established. I've spoken of my six lists as I pastored, and of the fact that people were trying to care for and pray for people they never saw regularly at church, which is possible in any church over 150.

By using the ABF system for congregational care, evangelism, Bible study, social activities, and pastoral care all become manageable because there is really one list! (Perhaps some churches will keep a separate membership list.)

Those who choose to stay out of congregational life can either be put on the care list of the appropriate ABF (someone chooses for them) or on a separate list. The latter will be necessary in the larger church over 1,000.

Some of these people will find their ties in a small cell; some will simply say, "We don't want any ties."

Models for ABFs or something similar are being used all over the country. Some churches actually use the term Adult Bible Fellowships. Many have adopted this method of reorganizing Sunday School electives, going carefully but slowly and surely. I hear reports that more caring and fellowship are happening.

One of the largest Southern Baptist churches in Houston builds all its caring and fellowship and outreach around the 150 adult groups that are a part of this huge church.

Then it is manageable.

Then the pastor can coach and pastor lay teachers and class leaders and care leaders, who share in the care of the people.

Growth happens by division. Each ABF can easily divide as it gets to a certain size, multiplying. (Admittedly, this is not an easy task because people who meet together for a while want to stay together and hate to lose their friendships, as they often say. Many times ABFs level off at about 80 or 90 because of this, and sometimes never to grow again.)

This will not be the source for fringe growth in the church, but certainly will be for involvement growth.

More leaders are produced. In each ABF leadership emerges or is trained for every facet of congregational life. That means lots of people help lead. It's not just the pastor.

Leadership in an ABF is unique:

• The leaders are selected not elected. Leaders for ABFs are selected by the leadership team for that group or by the pastor who advises that group. They are not the result of a vote for the one who's best up front.

• Leaders are selected by spiritual gifts and passions, not simply by being good in public. The care leader, for instance, is often somebody who does not like to be in public but who is very good at organizing and has a heart for people. The unit care leaders who take seven to ten families or units as their caring list are people who know how to touch lives, but perhaps do not teach well!

• Leadership is significant. The jobs are not busy work. They are people-work or outreach or socials or things that can really make a difference in the strategy of the church.

Fellowship is enhanced. Dividing the church into ABFs means offering something that produces friendships. It's one thing to have a "fellowship"—a stand up reception where people salute each other or nod a little or drink coffee or herbal tea for a few minutes! That can be a good start. But it's quite another to have them meeting with each other week after week, and even discussing subjects that interest all or most of them.

The best way to promote true camaraderie or fellowship is to study the Bible together and also adopt special projects together.

The church is made warmer. Any large church with over 90 adults is going to leave some unnoticed. There is certainly no magic to this ABF formula that means no one will go unnoticed, but it certainly adds to the possibility that people will know there's a group that wants them.

Every church over 90 has to have as one of its main goals to produce smaller groups where people can feel welcomed, grow in faith, and feel love. ABFs take the big bonfire, which only a few can get around, and break it up into smaller bonfires where there's room for everyone to feel the heat from the fire.

They help produce more warmth.

Outreach is strengthened. Instead of an outreach program aimed at the whole church, which many simply watch or cheer or criticize, each ABF has as part of its strategy some outreach to others for growth.

Yes there is ministry in cell groups. Yes you call for ministry in celebration groups. But in congregational life you have the planning of socials, the giving of gifts, the help when someone is ill or in the hospital, the caring related to divorce, the rescue related to financial devastation, and on and on.

Because so many needs are present and so much is going on in these many families or individuals, there is the need for spiritual gifts to be exercised.

Bible study is enhanced. You study best in an environment of friendship and continuity. While many churches love electives, the best applications usually happen in groups where you feel at home and where you know people and where you've already grappled with some things. I think this is one of the strongest advantages of ABFs. It's hard to help people get to know each other, and it makes it so much harder when they meet with one group on Sunday morning and another on Sunday evening and another on Wednesday and another in a home or another in a caring group. People just do not have time for so many friendships. So many of their groups may stay more superficial when it comes to real personal needs.

We can certainly learn Biblical truths through a lecture system or in electives. Content is important. But everyone needs a group where there is much more than that.

It's one thing if I am asked, "How does this verse strike you?" or even more specifically, "What do you struggle with in your own life about the love mentioned in this verse?" In a group where everyone is almost a stranger to me, I will give an answer that is not a lie but is certainly not the deepest issue of my heart or the most transparent thought.

But if I'm meeting with people that I know love me and that I have helped or been beside through a difficult time, I might talk about a sin or a struggle or goal of my heart right away. If I know this is a group that accepts truth and struggle, I might jump right in and talk about an incident that happened two days ago and how I blew it.

Bible study is best in an environment of friendship, especially when application and personal encouragement are some of the goals.

Study subjects can be better selected for the felt needs of the people. Electives can help that in many senses. People can elect the subject that they feel they need to study.

But division of the church into age groupings, at least approximately, and allowing the class leaders to select their subject, can be a strength for choosing subjects that are really needed for that group of people.

THREE

How ABFs Are Organized

ABFs teach caring and fellowship, but they also organize for it.

That was a big step for me — to organize. I had always preached loving and caring. I had tried to exemplify it also. I would give assignments to people, and hope they would carry through. Hope was the key word!

I remember one couple that was facing a special personal need, one that looked like a marriage difficulty, and I asked an active couple to call on them and see if they could befriend them. "Sure," was their response. A month later I remembered to ask the man who took the assignment if he had met this new couple. He had forgotten but would get to it.

Another few months. The new couple separated and would not talk about it.

I realized we needed to assign care and have a degree of accountability within a class or community, or it would not happen. This is when we started having the "class deacons" or "unit leaders," which is what we prefer calling them now. (The title "deacons" scared a few too many, and I also began to conclude that all the servant positions in the church could come under the general heading of deacons.)

These people must then give account every month to a care captain for the group, who asks certain things of them, and gives training and support to make their ministry possible.

At times I have heard the criticism that love-care that is assigned is not love at all. I do not agree with that.

If I were lying along the road after a car accident and a paramedic arrived in his ambulance, I would not ask him before he took me to the hospital, if he truly loved me. I would accept his help, assigned or spontaneous or whatever.

If a policeman stops to help me in a troubled time, I am not going to ask him to explain his motives. I'm just glad he was assigned to help.

I notice that people who help others through the church usually find acceptance. Love is appreciated. Besides, we've all been assigned to care for and encourage and love each other—by God!

I am not very good at assessing motives all the time or wondering why someone is doing something for me or others. I just want people to have their true needs met.

The fact is that after you show love to someone, assigned or spontaneous, your feelings for that person grow even stronger. Love bonds. And friendships are often lasting, even though they started with a brief hospital visit or a casserole delivered when there was a special need.

An Overview of the ABF Structure

This principle of assigning important responsibilities applies to the whole ABF organization.

ABFs are designed for fellowship, teaching/learning, pastoral caring, and outreach. All of these areas have managers who are responsible, and all of these managers relate to a staff pastor who carries the responsibility for that ABF.

A good ABF is organized so these vital functions can be carried out with excellence. It is not just a matter of throwing together a teacher, a classroom, and some students!

For sure there are varieties of organization. Especially in the area of caring, local leaders must be innovative and see what really works for them.

I believe the non-negotiables are these.

1. The Adult Bible Fellowships are not a separate ministry from the church. They are the main "congregations" within the church providing pastoral care, Bible teaching, evangelism, and small group discipleship.

No more of the separation of church and Sunday School!

2. The pastor is the main leader of the Adult Bible Fellowships. That does not necessarily mean he has direct involvement, but are a part of his overall plan for all the purposes named above!

The pastor becomes the senior leader and advisor for each ABF, which is then led by a class leader, a Bible teacher, and a care leader (and sometimes an outreach leader). These three or four (in some cases they are couples) are on an equal level and share responsibility for the class. Each has a clear responsibility. Each reports directly to a pastoral advisor for that class who unites his ministry to the whole church.

The pastor—the senior or other designated staff pastor—should take final responsibility. He should sense that adult education like this can care for so many of the "one another" commands put on him by the Lord in the Bible. He cannot just turn it over to the Sunday School. The ABF system must have his special interest and attention.

3. Each of the leaders has a clearly defined job description, with accountability and responsibility. So often people who have clear, written job descriptions at work get no directives at church or a nebulous "go to it." This should not be.

4. ABFs must be led by a team, not just by a teacher who feels this class is his own. Many Sunday School classes are organized so that a teacher is responsible not only for the lesson but also for all the direction of the class. Of course there are a few teachers who can do all this caring and worrying about more than the lesson, but not many. Certainly the teacher is naturally going to be the senior leader of the group, in most cases. But the healthiest leadership team will have several who carry the burden for the fellowship, the ABF.

It is essential that this group of leaders meet together as a team frequently. They must get to know each other and sense the direction of the class to help it get stronger. For complete job descriptions of these leaders, refer to the appendix.

Working with the pastor, the leadership team carries this ABF, this adult class.

A Close Look at the ABF Structure

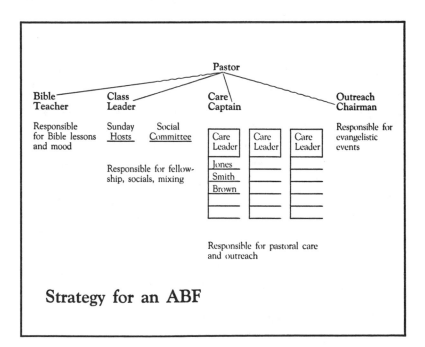

Strategy for an ABF

The chart says it clearly—there are three main leaders, sometimes four. Not one. Not the traditional teacher who stands alone and does everything (or doesn't do many things).

There are three! Maybe four.

The Bible teacher. He is responsible for the lesson and helping set the mood of love and study and application. He leads the lesson time and the evaluation of the lessons that the leadership team does. (Evaluation times at least every quarter can help the leadership team look hard at the class participation, mood, and subject matter.)

The class leader. He is appointed because he has a pastor's heart and because he is good in front of crowds, urging them to relate to each other and to relax. He also has good organizational skills to help plan socials and deal with other needs.

- *Social chairman.* This person (or couple) cares for the social needs and gets a committee working and many people involved. He or she understands that socials are not just to fill busy evenings, but rather to provide an essential environment for mixing and meeting new people.

- *Hosts.* These people greet others on Sundays and help them relax. Perhaps they assign or serve refreshments so that talking and relating go on easily.

A care leader. This person may never get up front, but he knows how to organize people for caring, and he wants to help. He is responsible for unit or care leaders who each take responsibility for five to ten families or individuals.

That responsibility includes prayer, help for special needs such as sickness or tragedy, concern for absenteeism, and encouragement toward spiritual growth and ministry involvement. The care leader is the manager and visionary for all this.

- *Unit leaders.* These are people who accept the pastoral responsibility to provide care for five to eight families or individuals. This couple or individual will need both nerve and love to take initiative to help others get involved, to "chase" absentees, and to listen and encourage.

  Sometimes these are outgoing aggressive types who major on group meetings, but no less effective are the quiet, even shy, types who regularly pray and systematically encourage and help others. What matters is that caring happens.

One goal I always emphasize for unit leaders is to pray for others in areas of character and spiritual life, not just wait for physical needs and surgery. God can help then, and prayer is needed, but strength can also come through prayer in moral and maturity areas.

The people assigned to these unit leaders can be regular attenders and newcomers. In the case of newcomers, the goal is to urge their involvement in the church or ABF. Some unit leaders feel comfortable calling new people and inviting them to try involvement or even have lunch and talk about the church. Others are better with just pastoral care.

Outreach or evangelism leader (an optional fourth leader). This couple or single helps keep evangelism in the minds of the ABF people and helps organize events that are conducive to involvement by new people and unbelievers.

We scheduled an elective course called "SaltShakers" (Thank you, Becky Pippert) and offered training and mutual encouragement in evangelism. Then the attenders were challenged to return to their ABFs to represent the evangelism emphases. In most cases that meant taking five or ten minutes in a class session to report on SaltShakers material and, more important, to tell of any personal attempts or feelings about sharing their faith with others.

Outreach events or socials suited for unbelievers should not be left to chance. Sports events or informal interaction at someone's house can include time for mixing and do not need the rather threatening idea of a devotional to persuade the new person or unbeliever. Each church must decide, but here's one churchman who favors no tricks—if you think you're going to a volleyball party, it should end up being a volleyball party, not that party plus a short "church service" or "evangelism program." Call it what it is. (There is nothing wrong with having a "church service" or "evangelism program" on a Friday evening in someone's home, but call it that if that's what it is going to be. A person who is tricked into a "church service" under the label of a volleyball party may never go to either one again.)

One of our target groups in some of our own fellowships has been unsaved or unchurched husbands. Most churches have approximately ten to twenty times as many wives who come without their husbands as vice-versa, and thus the concern to have some socials where they can attend without being threatened. Often these are men who have experienced first or second-degree burns previously when someone pushed them too hard at or about church, and they are consciously shy of church attempts.

The Leader of the Leaders

Under a normal arrangement, all of these main leaders report directly to the senior pastor or to a Christian education pastor or a staff pastor assigned to that ABF. That person is then the pastor the ABF leaders would turn to for special needs.

In a small church all of the ABFs may report to one pastor. In a larger church with several staff members, each pastor may be responsible for two or three ABFs, perhaps teaching one and advising the others.

My recommendation is to keep this pastoral connection strong. Remember, this is not just another ministry of twenty ministries at the church. This is the main church vehicle for congregational fellowship, accountability, relational growth, social interaction, and outreach. It is no small matter.

The pastor should speak about ABFs, give illustrations related to them, feature them in the services, and write to the people about them, including them in his "Note From the Pastor" in the weekly bulletin once in a while. For sure, it must be obvious to everyone that he really thinks this is not simply an appendix to the worship service, but a very vital avenue of growth.

Consider the following reasons why ABFs should be known and shown to be related to a pastor.

1. This stresses the importance of ABFs. Ministries that have the pastor as main visionary and manager are going to be considered more significant and closer to the heart of the church.

2. It gives visible pastoral care to people who are involved. Much pastoral care must be done by the "member-ministers" of the church, the individual believers who are called by the Lord to serve others in the name of Christ and to help build the body (Eph. 4:11-13; 1 Peter 4:10-11).

3. *It gives ABF leaders a clear system of accountability to someone who feels the burden of the whole church.* Not that laymen do not care about the broader picture of the church, but they are naturally not going to have the understanding of importance that the pastor who "eats and sleeps" the church has.

4. *From the pastor's viewpoint, this arrangement gives him a group of people to be his flock.* In a large church with more than one on pastoral staff, there can be confusion about who pastors whom. The lines should not be artificial or forced, but it helps to know that the people in a particular ABF or two or three ABFs are the people you should pursue, pastor, and disciple.

5. *A senior pastor or staff pastor can operate better with clearer and simpler areas of responsibility.* It can be confusing to have one list for pastoral care for deacons, another list of people who belong to various Sunday School classes, another list of newcomers, and perhaps even another for inactive members. In addition, many pastors have their own unofficial list of people they are pursuing for evangelism or discipleship.

That all makes too many lists.

As the church gets larger, with ABFs organized by age levels, it is natural for one staff pastor to have responsibility for young adults and all their ABFs, another for middle adults, and another for older adults.

In a very large church, one staff pastor might have the twenties, or even young twenties, another the thirties, another the forties, etc.

Of course there is much room for flexibility in all this. Each church easily adapts. One good thing about all the changes going on in our world is that some changes now come more easily. Fact is, many adult Sunday School classes could easily be moved toward this more complete arrangement. Elective systems can be run as new ABFs are started.

I believe the adage, "Most of us overestimate what we can do in a year and underestimate what we can do in five years."

FOUR

How ABFs Differ from Regular Sunday Schools

Many people hear the concept of the Adult Bible Fellowships, smile, and yawn their way back to regular adult classes.

Opening exercises, a nice class president who announces the next social, and the teacher. Then more of the teacher.

Adult Bible Fellowships are not the same.

Intention

Adult Bible Fellowships have organized fellowship and care and outreach into the study group that meets on Sundays—and these are not by-products. These are essentials in the fellowship and in the relationships.

Adult Bible Fellowships have a leadership team, multiple leaders, who help develop the caring system and the relationships within the group.

Adult Bible Fellowships are people who stay together to get to know each other, and to develop in their faith together.

Unlike electives, they are not people who meet together for a little while and study and then go away. Unlike the regular

Sunday School class, they are not just people who have a Bible study and sometimes throw in a social or two.

Adult Bible Fellowships are the way to honestly obey the "one another" commands of the Lord for us in the Bible. Many people have written chapters or preached sermons about these "one another" commands, but God is the One who commanded all of us earlier.

Love one another (John 13:34).

Be devoted to one another (Rom. 12:10).

Honor one another (Rom. 12:10).

Be united with one another (Rom. 15:5).

Accept one another (Rom. 15:7).

Admonish one another (Rom. 15:14).

Greet one another (Rom. 16:3-6, 16).

Serve one another (Gal. 5:13).

Bear one another's burdens (Gal. 6:2).

Bear with or forgive one another (Eph. 4:2).

Submit to one another (Eph. 5:21).

Encourage one another (1 Thes. 5:11).

Confess sin to one another (James 5:16).

Pray for one another (James 5:16).

Adult Bible Fellowships do not believe these things will happen spontaneously, or at least they do not leave them to chance.

ABFs organize the caring, the socials, the "cheers and tears" sharing parts of the hour.

Sunday Format

For years I sat through the "opening exercises" routine. Forgive me friends who helped me grow up, but I never got anything out of that ten or fifteen minute mini worship service. I feared the day when I would have to walk up front with my birthday offering, and I smiled inside when we sang, "Nine twenty-five, nine twenty-five, we will be in Sunday School at nine twenty-five." We always sang it at approximately nine thirty-five because we always started late.

I always knew that a lot of the people skipped opening exercises and were just down the hall waiting to go to class, or were already sitting in their classroom talking.

I remember in seminary my wife and I would get an extra ten minutes sleep on Sunday because the church we attended was right across the street and we could skip the opening time and we loved that. Or, finally some of us in the seminary couples class would gather in our Sunday School room and talk a little before Mr. Grant would start the lesson.

Maybe that was the beginning of Adult Bible Fellowships in my mind. The subconscious beginning, but indeed the seed.

In ABFs you go right to your class and have relaxed and spontaneous fellowship. People stand around with a cup of coffee or tea and talk. If your church won't let you have coffee, you might just want to hold empty cups because people talk better with a cup in their hand!

That's different from adult Sunday School.

Goals

The main goal of ABFs is to have people relate to each other—getting to know one another in the Word but also in real life.

The second goal, a close second, is Bible study and application to life. ABFs promote the idea that people who really love each other and know each other can study the Bible better together, and apply it with more integrity and directness!

The words I hear from people who have tried ABFs confirm the idea that it is different from the ordinary Sunday School. Not necessarily better. Not the only way. Not a new secret that has been discovered that Jesus never told. Just a solid method for helping groups of people—classes of people—come together in the name of Christ to really enjoy one another and grow in the Word and in the grace and knowledge of their Savior.

Yes, ABFs are different from the traditional Sunday School.

Structure

ABFs are an integral part of the pastor's plan. They report to him.

A whole leadership team serves with the pastor or staff leader to provide vision and management and love for this group. Success does not depend nearly as much on the teacher alone as it does in the classic Sunday School model.

Age Grouping

While some Sunday School classes are formed by various ages, many of them hope people will report to the next older class when they reach a certain age.

Other classes are grouped by elected subjects, chosen by the students for three months or two or one. Electives can be great, but just about the time you are getting to know others in the class and feeling okay about sharing openly, you move to another class and another subject.

ABFs usually just keep changing the posted ages for the classes as people mature in age.

Normally we create a new "Young Marrieds" class every year, allow it to keep that name for a year and then choose its permanent name. Then another new class can take the "Young Marrieds" name.

"All Church" Spirit

The adult program and youth program are not meant to be cousins or live-in neighbors or in-laws to the "regular" church. ABFs are the main caring and outreach arms of the church. They are usually not functioning under a different constitution or superintendent, or with a separate financial system. Many once functioned that way and others still do. It certainly is not suicide.

But it does seem so much more appropriate for ABFs to be the main assimilation, fellowship, study, discipleship, and outreach agency of the church.

When the pastor sees ABFs that way, it is much easier for him to invest time and support in them.

When other church leaders see the ABF system as such an important part of the church life, they help heal the schizophrenia that often exists and pitch in to help ABFs grow strong.

ABFs Enrich Congregational Life

Many of the Sunday School models in America have been for huge adult classes where someone teaches or preaches a lesson, and the people watch. While that may satisfy some, many adults desire friendships at church, not just sitting with people in the same pew. Congregational life is not going to happen in these celebration type services, no matter what they are called.

There must be a way for people to get to know each other and study and fellowship and socialize and reach out and minister on a long-term basis.

ABFs provide that.

A larger gathering must be treated in a whole different way than the medium-sized gathering. In fact, a gathering that is meeting only for six weeks or eight weeks must be treated all together differently than one that stays together over the long haul.

We have a "Pastor's Class" that meets for ten sessions, and even in that group of usually 50 people, relationships and friendships do not develop in a strong way. Of course a couple here or there may find an affinity with someone else and enjoy a continuing relationship, but normally, because it is so short, people do not form strong alliances in this class. Ten weeks or ten sessions are too short.

That's why I make the case against electives as a good means for fellowship.

Can regular adult Sunday School classes do the same thing as

ABFs for a larger church? Of course. In many ways an Adult Bible Fellowship is a regular adult Sunday School class! But when I use the term I am referring to the focus on caring, the multiple leadership, the outlook for outreach.

People will feel like they are a part of a small church in an ABF, or should. They will form friendships that everyone craves, be part of a caring unit where there is exchange of love and active ministry for each other, and have a natural opportunity for cell-discipleship experiences.

FIVE

How an ABF Brings
Health to a Church

Based on my own experience and other people's thoughts, I believe a healthy church will exhibit eight vital signs. And I believe the ABF system can help bring health in each area.

These healthy signs or strong vital signs for a good local church are certainly subjective, though none is lacking objective biblical command or principle.

The Sovereignty of God
God does everything He wills to do, and things happen the way He wants any time He directs (Eph. 1:11).

This vital sign means that one of the reasons churches grow is the sovereignty of God. He makes it possible. Sometimes two churches are in the same locale with the same methods, same heart, same kind of pastor, and the same love in the churches, and one grows and one does not.

In one sense — and I do not believe in fatalism! — what will be, will be, as God speaks. Job had it right: "The Lord gives and the Lord takes away."

46

And about the only thing we can do related to this health issue is pray and trust God.

So how do ABFs help?

Obviously, my answer is going to be nebulous on this one. ABFs can pray and trust God together!

But there really is very little anyone can do otherwise because sovereignty means sovereignty, and sovereignty is something that we people are not into!

I do like the manageable size of an ABF, and the fact that church leadership can call the people to prayer through this system in a much better way.

The Lordship of Christ

This growth concept or health sign for a church is related to obedience to Christ.

The pastoral leadership and main board of a church must lead the way here, obeying Scripture and using the pulpit to preach Scripture but also following Scripture when making committee and board decisions.

Christ is the head, the One for whom the church was made, and He is to be obeyed (Col. 1:18).

All of our churches would do well to restate this frequently and show by the style of preaching and the mood of obedience that we believe in it.

How do ABFs help with this?

For one thing, ABFs are a response to the Lordship of Christ. They help us all obey our Lord's frequent "one another" commands. We are to love one another and encourage one another and build one another . . . .

As Jethro once told Moses, there is no way for one pastor or even a few pastors to carry that out in a local church. Things must be organized and broken into manageable parts.

ABFs do that. The system provides realistic ways of fellowship and having community with each other. It also helps with a more manageable way for outreach and evangelism.

Of course, the whole purpose of meeting together is to honor the Lord and get to know Christ better in a congregational and love setting. Studying His Word with people you know and are

47

going to be with for a while is healthy and produces the real chemistry that aids the fulfillment of the "one another" commands.

The Leadership of Love
Healthy churches have leaders who love their people and show it. They watch out for them. They do it because they want to. Hebrews 13:7 and 17 and 1 Peter 5:1-5 call church leaders to shepherd with the heart of Christ and desire what is best for the people.

If you went to all the growing churches and spent some time or attended their seminars, you would see many different styles. Some would have a visionary pastor, others a chart-maker pastor who can show everything with amazing logic. Some would have a strong focus on the pulpit, others would feature an innovative style of worship. But one thing would be common: hard work and love from the leadership.

How do ABFs help with this one?

The ABF system was built to promote love. It is not a reaction to objective cerebral teaching so much as it is a reaction to classes for classes' sake.

ABFs have a system of teamwork that allows several strong opportunities to show love every Sunday. ABFs make room for more than one man to teach a class and say that he loves the class; they provide a team of leadership who love each other and love the class.

The teacher and class leader and care leader and outreach leader work together to lead with love. So do the hosts, care unit leaders, and people who plan socials and help people get to know each other. There is growing love.

We urge class leaders and others in addition to the teacher to get to know the people, to get new people involved, and to help build the people in the small groups. These leaders have many opportunities to express and show love — to say it but also to use their time to live love.

This love needs to start with the senior pastor. I recognize that. As the pastor builds a mood of love in the pulpit and expresses love to others who help lead, the ABF teachers and class leaders especially, that will filter down. People will adopt the same mood.

The Work of Many
Ephesians 4:11-15 talks about the passion of the Lord for the church—that everyone would be supplying strength and helping.

We use the term, "member minister" to refer to all those who join the church. I refuse to accept the term "minister" for myself though I realize this is just a matter of semantics. I prefer to be called a "playing coach" or a pastor, and I look at everyone in the church as ministers.

One of the secrets of a healthy church is that many do the work, not just a few.

How do ABFs help this health sign?

ABFs are created to help people minister.

In fact, one of the only weaknesses of ABFs that I have seen is that sometimes people work so hard in the ministries of their own ABF, building and reaching out, they are not available for ministries with children or youth. (I will address that weakness in Chapter 9.)

The work of many happens very well in the ABF system. It is not just the teacher who feels responsible for the class, but several other individuals or couples. In fact, it is not just these leadership people who feel responsible, but the caring and fellowship needs are passed down and given to many others.

The multiplication of ministry happens in many ways, especially as people who are in the ABFs get involved in small groups and regularly build into other lives. If they are motivated for fellowship and study at the ABF and they worship at the larger celebration service and they join a small group to get to know each other and have accountability, then the work of many is producing the growth of many.

I have seen many people who would be afraid to take a leadership job in the overall church become one of the care unit leaders for their peers or help with socials or outreach ministry in a particular ABF. As we all know, growth happens best in a ministry setting. If you do not drive your car, you do not have to go to a gas station. You do not need fuel. If you do not seek to minister to others and love them, knowing the Word of God is not nearly the felt need in your life. The ministry awakens the desire for the Word, and vice versa.

Former Oklahoma football coach Bud Wilkenson was once asked on national television, when pro football was just becoming "the national religion," what the rising interest in football had done for President John Kennedy's physical fitness campaign.

"Nothing," was his famous answer.

The announcer did not think Coach Wilkenson had heard the question so he asked it again: "What has the rising interest in professional football done for President Kennedy's physical fitness kick?"

"Nothing," was Mr. Wilkenson's reply again.

The announcer asked what he meant. And he received the answer that has been used in many sermons since: "Pro football is 22 tired men who desperately need a rest being watched by millions of people who desperately need exercise."

And that's the way it is in the church much of the time. If 15-20 percent of the people give 80-85 percent of the money, the same is true of workloads.

The ABFs try to counter this problem.

The Fellowship of Love

Ephesians 2:14-22 says that the doors are open at the church and that the walls have been broken down. Christ did this.

A healthy growing church promotes a mood of love throughout the fellowship. While it recognizes that most churches cannot meet the needs of all people, there will clearly be a mood of love with all the people who come.

How do ABFs help in this?

Quite obviously, ABFs are designed to cause love!

Love is not a feeling but an action, and ABFs have incorporated the actions of love in a group setting.

Strong ABFs care for their sick and needy. Good ABFs take care of even lighter personal needs. I know of one ABF where every woman who has a new baby is treated with a week of meals afterward. In one of our ABFs, church discipline has happened in the best sense, as two or three have gone to one to help bring restoration.

It is love in action.

People will not sense love in a personal way in a large church of over 100. They certainly will catch the mood of the church, and that's healthy. They will know that some of the people up front are there to hurt them or help them, to take advantage of their position or to minister to the people.

But ABFs can be where people feel love in a very special way. In these groups people respond to each other and get to know each other and are aware when someone is missing. ABFs are a natural for the fellowship of love in the church.

Some of our ABFs major on the "CPR" functions—caring and praying and relationships. Good. I am just as glad when they are built around Bible studies or just home meetings or accountability times. Whatever the focus, they can be very healthy.

The point is that love is happening in good ways.

The Outreach in Discipleship

The real command of the Lord in Matthew 28:19-20 is not just to evangelize, but to make disciples. Certainly His point was that a person who receives Christ should become a learner, a disciple.

51

But the point here is to use the word *discipleship* in an even more technical way, with the hope that a healthy church will not stop its evangelism efforts with "a decision," but will keep people growing and learning and being trained. The church growth people like to talk about disciples as people who have responsible church membership—people who really are included in the church and have found their place.

Whatever "magic" you attach to church, it seems obvious that receiving Christ requires more than just a head or heart decision.

What can ABFs do to help this?

ABFs include the teaching of discipleship and times of learning, usually at the main lesson times on Sunday. Each ABF is certainly built around the teaching time as well as the time for fellowship.

But the ABFs also provide a natural forum or skeleton for the forming of many discipleship groups. Manageable groups. Small groups are places where people can really share their hearts and encourage each other and admonish one another and grow together.

My personal opinion is that "decisional regeneration" is as bad as "baptismal regeneration" or "church membership regeneration."

A true decision is a decision to trust Christ and put your faith in Him, but it will grow. And the church must have the facilities—not buildings but groupings—for that growth.

ABFs can help.

Effective, Simple Organization with Accountability and Flexibility

If you read the writings of the Apostle Paul much, you get the idea that he wanted to make it simple to witness and do God's work. (1 Corinthians 9:22-23 talks about "being all things to all people" that some might be reached.) Sometimes church systems are so rigid that little gets done, or so free-wheeling that no one knows if anything is getting done!

A healthy church has simple organization. People know who is in charge of each area. Committees do not run everything since committees really do not run!

There are accountability and advisory groups, but people know what their jobs are and are allowed to do them.

How can ABFs help with this?

While I have emphasized team leadership for the ABFs, the charts clearly show that the senior pastor or pastoral staff member for the particular classes is the leader. "Wherever two or three are gathered together, one must be the leader," I always think.

But the job descriptions are very clear for all the leaders of an ABF. There's not a lot of red tape, at least there doesn't need to be. Responsibility should include the authority to get things done. The social chairman should be allowed to make some decisions and get the social planned and announced.

ABFs certainly help the health of the church because they simplify and centralize some of the systems. I began this book by saying that once I had six or seven lists of people as I pastored, and then brought it down to one main list through the ABFs. I have always appreciated the simplicity of the ABF system.

A Biblical Program Big Enough to Meet Needs

Church growth expert Carl George said in a lecture for pastors that a church as it grows must stop being a "Winnebago" going down the street and become many "small VWs" going down the street.

He means that churches need to be split up into many different groups and side doors and ways for people to be attached and involved in a network of friends. Not just one big congregation but many communities or congregations within the church.

People also need to be spread out in terms of interests or special needs. Some feel that only about 10 percent of the people in a regular church are healthy enough and ready enough for strong discipleship groups. Another 30 percent might be ready for relational groups or caring groups where people love each other and grow together that way. The vast majority of people might join a support group or an affinity group that deals with issues they are interested in.

So the church must help supply these groups for people who

are hurting in various areas or have special needs. Our "Mother's Club" meets on Wednesday mornings to help mothers of preschool children who feel the need for wisdom from others and to encourage each other.

Tuesday evening you might walk past the door where there's a Bible study for working women, and down the hall a group for alcoholics, and then in another section of the church a group for people with eating disorders.

Sunday night after church the adult children of alcoholics meet to talk about the Bible and their own lives and getting the two together.

Each church must see what the needs of the people are and then react or expand to meet those needs.

How do ABFs help in this way?

Certainly the whole point in breaking the adult program down into various groupings is to help meet needs and provide a variety of ways for people to fellowship within the church.

ABFs Help the Pastor Help the Church

In addition to strengthening the church in these eight vital ways, ABFs also strengthen the church by strengthening the pastor.

The pastor's job description in the Bible is clear but seems impossible to fulfill, especially in our culture. But ABFs can help.

• *Lead the church (Acts 20:28).* When I did this best I met with teachers and class leaders of the ABFs once a month. I do not do that anymore but would relish the opportunity if it could work in the size of church I now pastor.

I would give updates to all these people, help them hear my heart on the church, and remind them how much I appreciated them. They could then convey some of that back to their group. When they shared objectively and with lists, that was great. The news got around. My heart got around. But even if they chose not to do that, they would be "in the know" about church activities, strategy, goals. When things came up in their own ABF, they could explain or even argue, in the best sense, for a certain way we were going.

I lead better through this kind of delegation and organization, rather than just standing up in front of the whole church. Currently I try to do this through the pastoral leadership who then meet with their leaders.

- *Rule the church (1 Timothy 3:4-5).* Here the emphasis is on management, as you manage your own household. Being a pastor is not just standing in front of people or getting them to do certain things or follow Christ as you do, but it is helping organize the church.

Obviously ABFs are all about that. Management includes delegation or breaking down into workable sizes. It provides care and teaching and organization for each of the people who will want it.

- *Shepherd the people (1 Peter 5:1-4).* The common description of a pastor's job is shepherding. Studies and experience clearly show that no pastor can really shepherd or pastor more than 80 or 90 people. So if I'm going to stand before Christ with any kind of clean conscience about shepherding a church that is over 100 adults, I must have some way to do this, some way that helps the people know pastoral care is available, that someone is going to look out for them when they're in the hospital, that there is a good friend to call when they are in pain, and that a pastor will know when there is a tragedy.

I shepherd a church best through such flocks as ABFs.

I know there are many other ways to organize flocks—geography or zip code or in an arbitrary way or by electives—but most of this book argues for the need to be meeting together regularly, and that best friendships are formed with approximate same age.

- *Teach the people (2 Timothy 2:15).* Obviously one of the main responsibilities of the pastor-teacher is to impart the Word of God. Certainly that happens from the pulpit, but ABFs provide opportunities for this in the best setting from the lecterns.

- *Equip the saints (Ephesians 4:12).* Another responsibility of the pastor is to "mend the nets" of the people, to help them be healthy enough to be involved in ministry and in caring for others. The great paragraph about the church in Ephesians 4:12-16 calls for "every joint" (KJV) to do its part. Everyone is called to a way of ministry that will build up the body and get people involved.

This can be done from the pulpit and through any other communication from the pastor to the people, but there is no better experience ground than in the ABFs, among friends, where people can learn to minister and love and directly and clearly share with others.

I love the ABFs for the equipping strength they give.

Most church leaders in the churches I've served have been selected from people who began shining in their own ABF, who grew to strength of ministry by working in a smaller group like that.

• *Be an example (1 Peter 5:3).* The pastor is called to walk in front of the people and openly model what it means to follow Christ. For years I taught my own ABF, and this was a great way to be an example in an informal setting. All pastors who teach an ABF are going to have this opportunity—even more than in the pulpit.

So I am grateful as a pastor and church leader, for what ABFs have done for the two churches that have captured my heart. The advantages of ABFs show up every day in my schedule.

While this book is for all in adult areas of church life, not just pastors, it does present a system that can bring great personal satisfaction to the pastor himself. And it really does grow adults on Sunday mornings and during the week.

SIX

Starting ABFs

Where to begin?

Begin at the beginning, one class at a time, without loud fanfare but with a few trumpets and a few people who really believe in the idea.

And that belief will have to come after a time of meeting with you and thinking about it and deciding.

It will not happen overnight.

I have seen a few people bolt back from a seminar on ABFs and try to start one the next Sunday. And a year later when I see them at another seminar, they are discouraged: "Our people just didn't like the idea." Never to try again.

People hate change. People hate surprises. I've heard Lyle Schaller, my favorite church analyst and guru say that so many times. The first time I heard him say that I told him how good many changes are and asked why in the world people wouldn't enjoy those changes. He told me to sit in a different chair in my home the next day when I went back.

"How did you know that I always sit in the same chair?"

"Just try it," he said.

When I did, my oldest daughter came down and asked, "What's wrong?"

Daughter number two, as she came down for breakfast, said, "Dad, you're in my chair. Get out."

We changed chairs, and we never changed again since.

People do get into ruts and hate changes.

So you don't want to throw a new church concept at people and start right in. Actually the changes to an ABF from a normal adult Sunday School class are in some cases subtle. But they are real. I remember the first time I urged a class to stop their annual election for president of the class. They were electing one of the nicest men, but certainly not one that had a heart for the kind of thing we wanted an ABF to do!

"We've always elected a president," one man told me. His words aren't hard to remember. He was very clear.

I persisted in this case, but I also went slowly with other classes and gradually we had about 14 ABFs, each with an appointed class leader and care leader as well as teacher, all of whom worked as a team with a pastoral advisor.

In the church where I am now we have about 30 ABFs, with some variety in arrangements, but with the same principles of care and fellowship and congregational life.

We started with one model. Wes, our minister of family and counseling, still considers his ABF *The Model* for our church, and I agree.

So start slowly. Start with one person, who will manage the project with you. Gather the other leadership positions for an ABF or take the present leaders and show them how a few changes and a new emphasis can move the class toward a more caring system of love and social life and fellowship as well as teaching.

These people need to believe in ABFs and own the project with you.

This is no place for a solo flight, and neither are any church changes. Stand alone if you wish to fight for the deity of Christ or the inspiration of Scripture, but not for the forming of an ABF!

People will enjoy the change and believe in it after they see the principles and how it works.

Timeline for Beginning a New ABF
For the sake of the calendar, consider beginning an ABF on September 2, after taking the following steps.

February through April—The decision is made to begin an ABF in September.

Immediately, or April—Begin leaking the news that there will be a new ABF and approximately what the age is or the subject.

April—Begin talking to the key couples for the class, people who will consider class leadership, care leadership, and teaching.

May—Confirm the leadership and begin developing others to assist them in beginning the class, behind the scenes.

June—Have at least 10 or 15 other people, confirmed to help begin the class, talk about it with their friends and meet together to pray for the class and decide on the first subject and the timing.

July—A main announcement should be made in the church mailing and from the pulpit. The date is announced.

July/August — Constant announcements should begin about the beginning on September 2.

July/August — Now constant announcements about the first subject to be studied should be made. Usually you pick a topical subject to interest people of that age group. For instance, a study about the initial years of marriage for young marrieds. Or something on teenagers or an empty nest for those in their middle years. This of course depends on the size of the church.

September 2 — Begin the class.

September 9 — Celebrate the beginning of the class in church, and in prayer.

Time Format for a 9:30–10:35 Session
Consider the following schedule as you launch your first ABF.

9:15	Hosts begin greeting.
9:30	People gather and relax. This is a time for coffee and tea and greetings. The leadership team helps new people relax, and they walk around to set a mood of friendship.
9:40	Opening welcome, announcements, requests. Led by the Class Leader, this is the time to introduce new people, pray for one another, and have several people share news or feelings. Some of this is planned and some is spontaneous.
9:50	The lesson. Forty or 45 minutes is plenty of time to learn and adopt a good lesson.
10:30	Closing prayers or invitations to any all-church events, or worship service announcement.
10:35	Dismissal.

A Closer Look at the Format

Gathering. It's important that preparations be made for the environment of the class, to promote fellowship and relaxation. The class leader or someone he designates should have the room set up for coffee or tea or water. (Many of us believe that even if you hold a cup of air in your hand, conversation will be better).

Some fellowships like to have the chairs arranged in moonshape, semicircle type arrangement so that discussion happens more easily. Others prefer to keep the chairs up against the wall so that people walk about and talk the first ten minutes, and the atmosphere is more relaxed. Sometimes when the chairs are all set up people will go directly to their seats without socializing.

Opening. Usually the class leader will begin the session and call people to order. Normally this is a very special time with the following ingredients:

1. *Welcome everyone.*

2. *Welcome special guests.* It is always best if people will introduce the friends they brought and say a word about them. Usually a brief applause as at Rotary meetings, helps people relax.

3. *General announcements.* This is the place where people can relax with announcements and not be hurried as in a worship service. Usually someone gets up and tells about the next social or even gives a report on the last one. Perhaps there are some small-group Bible studies arising out of the class that need to be announced.

4. *"Cheers and tears."* This is a time when the class leader asks people to talk about any special things in their lives or specific prayer needs. Usually it's best if one or two people are prepared to share a minute or two each about something. That primes the pump for others.

A caution: often this time turns into a listing of hospital stays and broken bones. And those are fine as prayer subjects, but it would be better to major on deeper issues and special needs.

Another good thing to do in the opening is to feature one single or couple, having them tell a little bit about where they work, how long they've been in the church, and their family.

The real purpose of this whole time is to help people relax

61

with each other, get to know each other, and develop a foundation on which to better fellowship. All of this is biblical!

The lesson. Here the teacher takes over and gets the people into the Word.

The closing. Either the teacher or class leader or some designated person closes with a prayer related to the lesson and its application to life. (But not a three-point prayer reviewing the lesson—God does not need that with His memory!) It is good to send them off with warm words.

How It Really Works: An Example
This could be a typical 9:30 A.M. ABF session.

9:13 Jim and Ann, class leaders for the Truth Seekers ABF, arrive in the room. They take up some of the chairs at the back and put them on the side. They move a wastebasket from right in the center of the front to a corner.

9:15 Sally, a single mother, arrives. She is the class host, Jim and Ann have asked her to do this, and she has felt much more a part of the church since then. She makes the coffee. She looks at her watch because the class greeters are not there yet. She expresses a little worry to Jim and Ann.

9:20 Four of the class greeters arrive, having met in the parking lot and walked in together. They have name tags, and they get over to the door in a few minutes to help welcome people. One couple stands at the door and the other stands over by the coffee pot to help people feel at home and meet others.

9:23 The first couple arrives. The Jennings, standing at the door, greet the couple and urge them to get inside to help greet others since the Jennings know them well.

9:24 Other couples and singles begin arriving and head toward the coffee pot.

9:30 Nothing official happens. People are standing around. Class leaders and hosts are mixing and trying to welcome three new people who happened to come this week—one brought by a couple who is walking them around to introduce them to others, and the others wandered in having seen the name of the ABF on a chart that is in the bulletin every other week.

9:35 Jim uses his loud voice to call the class to its seats. He is not worried that it is five minutes after the starting time. This class started at 9:23! He's glad the people are mixing and talking a lot. He knows that will help as they sit down.

9:36 Jim speaks over the buzzing and finally people pay attention.

"Let me tell you something pretty wonderful!" he gets their attention. "God has answered the prayers of our country and the world related to the war in the Middle East. Let's thank Him before we do anything else today because we've been praying about this for a long time. And as we do, let me remind you that Carol and Bob are celebrating because their son is going to come home in three weeks they think. Right, Carol and Bob?"

Carol and Bob have had a son in the war, and Bob shares something of their feelings. Jim asks for two people to lead in sentence prayers to thank God for that.

9:38 Jim says, "What other 'cheers or tears' do people have to share this week—something that has been especially joyful in your life or especially painful."

Fred Lentz raises his hand and shares something related to his job loss but how God has provided some consulting work that could go on for several months. (Actually Jim had heard about this and asked Fred to be ready to start this sharing time by explaining what he and his family are going through.)

His words open the way for several others to talk about something especially joyful or painful. Because they have heard others be candid on other Sundays, it is not as hard or threatening to talk at the beginning of class.

9:46 Jim mentions, "All kinds of things are happening in our lives—that's for sure. That's why we meet and want to study God's Word and apply it to daily living. Thanks for sharing your hearts and being a part of this family. Let's pray together for a few minutes as we remember these needs. Can I ask one of you who is sitting near someone who made a request to just say a sentence asking for God's grace?"

There are several minutes of prayer, and quietness, but a number of people lead out in sentence prayers.

"God, please help Fred get a job soon, but thank You for the way You are helping him face this."

"Thank You, Lord, for the peace that we have with You through Jesus Christ."

"Thanks for the kind of church that cares about each other, and thank You for this group where we find acceptance and a sense of love."

"Help us to learn more about Your Word today, especially these verses ahead here in 1 John. I pray for the kind of assurance we talked about last week."

"Lord, thank You for Don and for his teaching ability, and I pray You'd help us see what You want us to do and be as we look at Your Word today."

Jim closes the prayer: "Yes, thank You, Lord. We give You this hour for study and for wisdom that comes from You. In the name of Christ we pray. Amen."

9:52 Don moves to the overhead projector and people open their Bibles to 1 John 2. The lesson begins.

Normally the teacher will teach the way he does best. Some will lecture. My hope is that these ABF sessions will be much different from a sermon. I hope that the first 20 or 25 minutes of this lesson time will focus on teaching but that application and questions would also be included then or especially in the last 15 or 20 minutes of the lesson time.

Some teachers will teach for 20 minutes and then break the group into smaller groups of six to ten to answer some assigned questions that apply to the text or give help in understanding.

Certainly the personality and habits of the teacher will determine this, but also the goals and philosphy of the church.

Granted, it will not happen overnight, but it can begin.

One old motivational set of questions asks it well:

"If not you, who?

"If not now, when?"

SEVEN

Making Sure ABFs Work

A long time ago I learned four key steps with which to evaluate an Adult Bible Fellowship or any other group. Or the church itself.

They are simple, helpful.

1. *Getting people there: are people coming?*
2. *Receiving them: how are they welcomed?*
3. *Assimilating them: do they make friends and feel at home?*
4. *Discipling them: do they become productive and active follow-ers of Jesus Christ, trained to minister and help others?*

Let's look at these steps in a general way and then as they relate to ABFs. The four questions become a great way to assess how the church is doing with people. They are an especially important way to ensure that ABFs will work.

Getting Them In: Are People Coming?

It's pretty simple. Are we getting people to come? Are we get-ting them in?

Most people come in the side door of the church with a

friend. Most statistics show that over 80 percent of the people who attend a church the first time come through a side door—a concert, a special event, a special service, or a friendship. Very few people check the yellow pages to find a church that's having services Sunday or read the church page ads and say across the dinner table, "Honey, look, here's a church that's having services at 9:00 and 11:00 next Sunday—let's go!"

But they might come to an ABF volleyball social or to the Monday night basketball league, or to the Christmas Concert or to a discussion about parenting. They might play on the softball team, or their child might come to a Neighborhood Bible Club or to a special music event. Those are side doors to the church.

Any church or group needs to analyze how people come. The day is long gone when you simply had to advertise a program.

Someone has said that the languages of America are sports and music, so some of the side doors to the church need to be in these areas. Certainly there is also a huge felt need in the area of parenting. Our church has had wonderful success, as have many others, with a Mother's Club designed to give instruction and motivation for mothers of young children. Parents of little children are so concerned, and helping them can be a wonderful way to introduce them to the church.

So churches must analyze how they get people to come.

Adult Bible Fellowships must do the same. Maybe "pack a pew" works some places, but not where I've been. Not anymore. There must be an invigorating environment, a place of joy and aggressive application and study that makes people want to bring their friends.

A shotgun approach to growth in a local church brings some results, but focusing on specific target groups is a better approach. The strategy for ABF growth can focus on some clear special groups:

Friends of the "growers." "Growers" are usually those people who are fairly new to the class and to the church, and often to the Lord. They are excited about their faith, and they want to share it. In addition, they still have connections with people who are outside the faith and the church.

Help them bring friends! Encourage it! These are usually the people who will bring their neighbors to socials, or even to the special elective subject that may be in the ABF.

Studies show that within a year or two, people who have joined Christ and the church no longer have any unbelieving friends outside the church. The good thing that has happened in their lives is that they have become friends with believers who have helped them mature. The bad thing is obvious—they have dropped connections with the very people who need the message they now endorse.

So in the early months of ABF involvement, a primary target group can be the people known by these "latecomers." This would mean that the leadership should include teaching on the subject of friendship evangelism, helping people be free to relate to old friends and not so enclosing them in the church that they no longer have connections or time for unbelievers.

Specific target groups. It seems much easier as well as more fruitful to form a ministry or have a target group for a specific kind of person. For instance, have an affinity group, an evangelism thrust, for medical people. Or have a speaker or a monthly meeting or a special kind of service for business people.

Our Chapel Business Club began as a way to gather people at a meeting that will at least introduce our faith and give them a chance to have healthy conversation about it with Christians as they leave or some time later.

ABFs can sponsor such a gathering or a social aimed to attract a certain group of people. Perhaps "people who like volleyball" are not quite a target group according to Frank Tillapaugh's "unleashing the church" philosophy. Still, the more an ABF in a church can concentrate on reaching specific groups and appealing to them with specific presentations, the stronger it will be.

An ABF might develop a four-week elective on managing finances and the home, or raising teenagers. Perhaps three weeks of debates on particular issues might get some interest from adults who could then fit into that ABF.

Fringe people in the church. Many people who regularly attend church or become official members are not certain about their faith and know little about the Bible. I'm always grateful that such people come to church. In fact, sometimes I grow impatient with people who grow impatient with them! "I'm just glad they're here," I always defend them.

But these people should be a target group for the ABFs, where they will be put into a web, cared for, and befriended. Some of the people you hope to reach are ten blocks away or ten miles away, and their best connection is their friend who attends. But some of the people you should reach are sitting right in your own auditorium or sanctuary.

In one informal study and one formal study, the answer to the question, "Why don't you go to Sunday School?" was pretty simple. "Nobody has invited me."

Receiving Them: How Are They Welcomed?
This is the step any church or adult group can take without special training or a lot of money or specialization, but often it is neglected.

I was visiting in a church in Wheaton, Illinois, that rather "holy city" of America. My wife and I were looking for a class to attend, but there were no greeters to welcome us. I began greeting people in the hall, "Welcome to ——— church."

"Stop that," my wife said.

But I felt somebody had to do it.

It's so easy for a church to pray that visitors will come, hope that visitors will come, announce that visitors should come, and then do nothing to welcome the visitors when they come.

In another church I attended on vacation two greeters were talking to each other as I walked by. They were holding bulletins but having eye contact and enjoying each other. An usher who was closer to the sanctuary was actively involved in a discussion with someone he knew. The people in the pews were all in the back half of the church and all at the ends of the pews, daring someone to sit in front of them or making someone climb over them to get into the pews.

That kind of setting is not visitor-friendly!

"Receiving them" means help in the parking lot sometimes. It certainly means greeters at the doors. It certainly means clean restrooms and nurseries.

How do you decide whether or not you will return to a restaurant after you visit it once? Probably by the way you are received. And the cleanliness of the restrooms. And the service from the servers. And the content of the food!

There are times I eat at a restaurant or make a purchase at a store when I feel like the server is saying to me, "What are you doing here?"

That hardly seems the purpose for a restaurant or a church.

Some friends of mine visited a church in the west where someone met them in the parking lot, gave them directions about the church building, and invited them to dinner after the services. If they hadn't lived about 38 hours away from the church, they probably would have started going there.

ABFs are assigned a classroom. But chairs and blackboards and overheads and lecterns are not enough. One of the main duties of the class leader is to appoint a class host and greeters to man the doors and help people feel at home.

It should be a mortal sin for someone to walk into an ABF room without being greeted, introduced to others, and made to feel at home.

Again I say, this is the easiest step to correct. But it is often the most neglected.

If I were making a visit to a Zembo Mosque, and there was one when I grew up in Harrisburg, to attend a special service of the Shriners on Thursday evening, I would be nervous. I would not know what to expect. I would not know what to do when I got in there.

My perception of the Shriners has something to do with tall red fez hats, some horses in a parade and the good they do for children. But I certainly have no idea what I would expect at a service.

People who have not been to church for a long time come with the same fears if they come at all. What will happen? Will they feel at home? How will people receive them?

Every ABF leadership team should sit down and decide how people will be received when they get there.

Once in awhile when I speak at another church, I put the pastor through a bit of tension when he and I talk about what we will do just before the service. The normal thing is for the people to come in and sit down while the pastor hides in his office for prayer, ready to walk out at the last minute before the service begins. I sometimes suggest we stand at the door and greet people as they enter the sanctuary.

This is the one day in the week when people come to where these pastors are! It is the one day in the week when all the people we are trying to get to know, or at least many of them, show up in one room. And then sometimes we hide in prayer or in solitude while they are there. Obviously, I think it's important to get out there and touch them and meet them and greet them and welcome them.

One of the reasons for having a class leader and a class host, not just one teacher who feels responsibility for a particular class, is that this frees people to concentrate on only one task. Hosts should have no other passion than to meet these visitors and help all who are coming to feel at home.

When that happens, people may return.

The content of the lesson is important: relaxation and enjoyment of other people is significant. But first impressions may be the most lasting! Receive them well!

I met a couple a few weeks ago who had not been to church for 15 years. Can you imagine their feelings as they walked into the building? I am sure they had butterflies and wondered what

would be happening. "Is this going to be any fun? What's this place like? Will I get burned like I did when I was little?"

One of the main assignments for a class host is to help visitors meet someone with whom they might have an affinity — same kind of job, same age children, same interests. Perhaps a racquetball appointment can be made right there at the beginning of class.

"Receiving them" — an important way to make an ABF work.

Assimilating Them: Do They Make Friends and Feel at Home?

Assimilate is a hard word and a harder process. It is a catch word among people who study church growth, and it should be.

Assimilating people means helping them join a network of friends, helping them feel at home, making sure that they are received into a network of others.

One of the great problems in most churches is that the people who plan activities or assess the church and its adult groups are very busy people. Sometimes they turn down the idea of a picnic or a sports event or a special social, for instance, because they are so busy.

I want to scream, "The event is not for you! It is to help people be received and assimilated!"

This event is intended to be a side door to the church for people who do not come to the regular class or who do not relax when the Bible is being studied. It is imperative that leaders make sure that plans like this which might help a church with assimilation are not made by people who already have their nets full of friends.

If you can only have 4 or 5 very close friends and 10 or 12 really good friends, your nets may be full. You may not want to include anybody else in your circle; therefore you will not be a good help and strength for someone coming into the ABF or church.

Sometimes people walk into a church with a clear agenda and sometimes just with the normal human needs. Either way, they will walk out the back door a few months later if they do not make friends. One survey and study by Win Arn of The Institute for American Church Growth says that if someone does not make seven new friends in the first year at a church, he's gone. (Such studies are usually based on surveys of people who have left churches, and they are pretty accurate.)

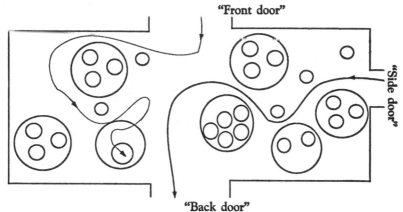

"Front door"

"Side door"

"Back door"

People who enter the church through the "front door" (main services) or "side door" (special events, support groups, or socials) need to be caught up in one of the webs of the church or they will usually go out the "back door" of the church. Sometimes when they do that they are not even missed, especially in a church over 200.

And ABF structure is designed to latch on to new people with love.

The number one reason people choose to keep going to a church is: "I feel accepted." Dr. David Jones, a researcher in Jackson, Mississippi says, "People are looking for a group of individuals who will first and foremost make them feel accepted" (*RD Digest,* January 1985).

My contention is that unless people are trained to assimilate others they do not do it very well. It's more than saying welcome. There are many ways to talk about receiving people. Some Christians need to be freed up simply to include non-Christians in their network. Others need to be challenged to reach out more to new people.

I remember talking with a group of ladies who had met together for eight years in a Bible study — just the eight of them for eight years. I urged them to break it up—I didn't say it so bluntly—and each start new groups with others. But they were too attached to each other.

Assimilation of new people is hard work. Even for those who really love others and love Christ.

One church I knew had auditorium hosts, people assigned to certain places in the auditorium to meet newcomers in that area. I think those auditorium hosts should leap over pews after the benediction to get to the visitors and welcome them.

ABFs need such people. They usually are the unit leaders, who know that part of their job is to welcome new people and try to get to know them.

The main assimilation of someone into an ABF can be done by a unit leader who has been trained to ask the right questions of people. The unit leader might invite a newcomer to lunch or dessert or to do something that is not threatening but clearly shows acceptance.

The class leader and the care leader should lead the way on this issue. The sensitivity of the class leader as he opens the ABF session is important. There are ways to "rush" a visitor and put too much pressure on at first. There are also ways to warmly have friends introduce visitors they've brought.

Assimilation needs to be taught. And caught. A church takes on the mood of its leadership. As I write this, I have just returned with my wife from speaking at church about two hours from where we live. We both remarked immediately after the service how friendly the people were.

As we sat with the pastor and his wife we thanked them for their own friendliness, which is duplicated by their people.

Leadership reproduces after its kind. Jesus said something like that in Luke 6:40.

How do your Sunday School classes or ABFs, if you choose to call them that, rate in the area of assimilation of new people?

If new people visit a church or a class largely due to friends inviting them or walking through "side doors," they go back the second time because of the way they were received and they keep going to that place because of the way they were assimilated!

Discipling Them: Do They Become Productive and Active Followers of Jesus Christ, Trained to Minister and Help Others?

This is the hard one sometimes.

There is a great difference in people and the speed at which they learn and get involved and the motivation that gets them moving. Every coach knows that. Of the 12 players on an NBA basketball team, each one is motivated to work hard in a different way. Some basics must be assumed, but other ways of teaching and leading become very personal as the coach gets to know what pushes and motivates and guides each player.

The same is true in the church.

But the end result is clear: "Make disciples" (Matt. 28:19). God certainly did not have that written so we would spend our time debating how strong a disciple a person must be before he is forgiven. The point is, all who are in Christ are disciples and should be growing. This rules out an evaluation of a church by sheer numbers.

There are many wonderful programs of discipleship, and sometimes I believe that the content is almost an excuse for people to get together in a small group for discipleship—let me quickly explain!

The booklet used or the expertise of the leader in going through the Scriptures and applying them may not be as important as the fact that people are working on their hearts and habits and using Scripture and trusting God's grace and Spirit to dig up weeds and grow fruit within them. That is the issue. That is discipleship.

Everyone in the church should have the opportunity as well as the instruction and the motivation to be discipled personally. But a person will do exactly what he chooses to do.

I used to carry such guilt, or at least a special burden, for people that if they did not grow, I took it personally. There are people who will be a part of church if you visit them or call them each week, or they will grow more in their faith if they get the content or motivation directly from the senior leader.

It's important for church leadership to do everything possible, to motivate, to love. But it is also important for every churchman to believe that "everyone does exactly what he wants to do" in this area. It was Abraham Lincoln who said, "Everyone over 40 is responsible for his own face."

There may be exceptions, but the issue is clear: offer the help and grow yourself, but then help people be accountable directly to God!

In the ABFs, training and discipleship have a head start. Why not be discipled among friends that you meet with each Sunday? Why not have your more specific training or ministry motivation or accountability groups grow out of the "congregation" that you meet with regularly? These people are your friends, and it's hard enough to make friends in one group of church, let alone two or three.

The ABF is a natural setting for developing small groups. These groups may be the units lead by the "care leaders" or "unit leaders" who are responsible for four to eight families or singles. The groups may meet together twice a month for personal growth together or accountability. Often the focus of these groups is not so much a lot more content as applying what has been learned previously.

Here in small groups, people can be trained for a special mission of the ABF. Perhaps an ABF can take on a certain ministry for a missions conference, or adopt a missionary, or teach in a certain department of the church. Training for these ministries can happen within the ABF a little, and then be followed up in the small groups that happen during the week.

I often use the four questions in this chapter to evaluate a group in the church to see how it is doing. The questions can be an excellent discussion agenda for a brief retreat for the leadership team of an ABF or any group.

I'm glad I learned them.

EIGHT

Reasons Why ABFs Don't Thrive

It seems so simple. Several times I've heard church growth experts talk about the number one reason people don't go to Sunday School or to Adult Bible Fellowships: nobody invites them.

So often I have mentioned ABFs from the pulpit and then been hit with a reminder, *not everyone knows what an ABF is.* We use our monograms and abbreviations and little letters that are so clever and so much a part of our vocabulary, but new people or visitors won't understand them. And we never even mention the whole program, thinking that everybody knows what's offered here.

Go into a restaurant and they tell you about their specials first thing!

Our church averages a large number of visitors every Sunday, most of whom would not know an ABF class from an ABF truck. Publicity is needed. Explanations.

The tension comes from the time we allot to this because we do not want to be offering commercials in the worship services.

The facts can be made known in mailings and with sermon illustrations and with brief moments of announcements.

Writing this makes me want to do better!

I really believe people need to be in smaller groups. I really believe that it's biblical to have the kind of connections you can have in an ABF, with true fellowship and lasting encouragement. Let's do everything we can to keep ABFs alive and healthy. As you read in this chapter about other reasons for weak ABFs, I hope you will vow to avoid these problems in your own church.

No Accountability Is Required

All of these organizational charts look fine on paper. But each ABF, each organized class, needs someone serving as advisor or giving accountability checks or making sure that there is progress in various areas. So often I have given my talks and even trained the leaders and then checked back in a year to find that little has been done in certain areas. I believe each ABF needs a staff advisor or someone who's going to really work to help the group follow the standards. Not that there cannot be flexibility, or changing of the job descriptions to meet their real needs. That's fine. Whatever works, works.

But usually whatever is not checked, will not work. What's the famous slogan, "People do not do what you expect but what you inspect"?

Monthly teachers' meetings may be harder in today's society with crunched schedules. But some kind of accountability and occasional group meetings are very important.

Young Marrieds Are Only Slightly Touched

Often churches can do well with this whole system with people 30 and over, but miss the wonderful experience this can be for the young marrieds. It may be harder work to get them to an ABF.

Normally they are not going to come at an early hour.

They will not come unless a friend brings them, at least in many cases.

They will not come if the subject matter is always Ezekiel or

Hebrews, and never subjects that really interest them.

Most churches with a degree of growth should start a new young married's class on a regular basis — every year or every two or three years at least, calling it "young marrieds" for awhile so people know where to come and then changing the name to something that does not indicate age or marriage status. (That's how every church gets a "Bereans" class and "Ambassadors" if they do not already have a "Pathfinders.")

The Teacher Merely Salutes the ABF System

Some ABF teachers will not allow the other leaders to help set the mood or really get involved in the whole program of fellowship or discipleship.

Many teachers are like that. They want to teach a lesson, will take a full 50 or 55 minutes for that if they can, and feel like the people are being cheated when the teacher is not standing up and exegeting or applying the word of God. Thank God for the passion of such a heart!

But somewhere the teacher must be educated or discipled or merely ordered to see that relaxing and socializing and hearing about each others needs and cares can help teaching go even better. I am convinced of that. Learning is best in an atmosphere of warm relationships.

All of this is why I prefer to call all three leaders of an ABF equals, though I understand that a teacher, by virtue of time up front or heart for the Word, is going to be considered the senior leader of the class.

Helping the teacher understand his role is certainly the responsibility of the pastoral advisor for the ABF or the pastor of the church. That can be very difficult.

One of our teachers obviously did not like the new emphasis on fellowship and the call to take some minutes at the beginning of each class to relate to each other. I remember his response on one occasion when we were having all of the ABFs represent their ministries and describe their main mood and what age group they represent — we called it "an ABF fair." This teacher would not call his class an ABF, but put in a very strong way on the poster, "A good old-fashioned Sunday School class."

Leaders Are Not Patient Enough

Sometimes people try to begin ABFs overnight and that never works. At least this method doesn't produce a healthy, growing adult group.

Someone has said, "We should be very shocked if we don't realize how little we can do in a year and how much we can do in five years."

Often we give up.

In most organizational transitions to a new leader there is something that tests our leadership or the good of a program in the second or third year, and by the fourth year then you're ready to take over.

Some ABFs Get Ingrown

Sometimes 20 or 30 people like each other so much that they do not want to grow and do not work to reach out to others.

Here I would simply want to take the teacher and the class leader and care leader aside and talk about what the Scriptures say and why growth could be very healthy. They are the ones that are going to have to change the mood and cause a new interest.

Teaching Is Entirely One Way

Too much lecture can be too much lecture. Too much discussion the same. Variety is important.

But each ABF teacher must be allowed to develop his own style and to be himself. Certainly, variety seems like the best answer for this, and people do want to be involved. One of the advantages of the smaller group, whether it's 50 or 60 or 30, is that there can be interaction. People know each other. They're not afraid to raise questions.

A sermon is a sermon. It is one man proclaiming. So ABFs certainly should be different from that—at least at times. Sometimes ABFs can get so big, especially for singles or college age, that they become a duplicate of the morning worship, or at least a parallel with more flavor for that particular age group. Some people in that age group then drop out of the main worship service and attend only their special part of the church.

There are so many good guides for teachers about methods.

Elmer Towns, longtime expert on Sunday School, has written that there must be three things to make a good Sunday School hour for adults:

1. A coffee pot—to stimulate fellowship.
2. An overhead—to show the outline and help content.
3. Questions—to get people involved.

Relationships Won't Happen Spontaneously

I have quoted a number of times the surveys that show that people come to church, especially the Sunday School part, more for relationships than anything else. It is truly a felt need. If we assume that relationships and friendships and caring and bonding will happen spontaneously, we make a mistake.

I have often assumed that because I've preached on something, it's happening. Not true.

I have often assumed that everyone in a class feels the same way I do about caring relationships and the need to welcome people and will move out of their shells or networks of close friends to include the new people. Not true.

There are many people in all of our churches who work very hard to include new people. But there are many who do not. And a new person can easily get missed.

I received a letter that made me cry. It was from a man who was single and had come to our church at least six times and had not felt welcomed. He even went to an ABF. Finally someone hit his car in the parking lot after the third service. His letter moaned, "Finally I got noticed."

Caring needs to be assigned just as evangelism does at times. Everybody should do it and some do a little, but some need to have it as a major priority.

Each Adult Bible Fellowship or adult Sunday School class should have certain people designated to welcome (hosts) and to pastor and shepherd the people (unit leaders). We're not talking about a caring or shepherding that does too much with people or tries to obligate them in ways they do not want to feel obligated! But caring needs to be assigned.

One of the early things any church leader should do is be sure there are greeters and hosts and people who help you feel wel-come when you get to the class or the church.

The parallel with a restaurant is a good one—there are not only servers who bring the food, but people who host and help you feel welcome and care for other details.

Not Enough Responsibility Is Given to the Lay Leaders

Often, in spite of how many people are included in the chart on an ABF, one person does most of the work. Usually it is the staff person or the teacher.

People will respond to a challenge. People like to help. People like to feel needed. They do not like to do unnecessary jobs or fill in time. But they do take up the challenge if they feel it is worthwhile. Therefore they need to know exactly what they're doing and why they're doing it and perhaps see someone else do it before they do it.

"I do; we do; you do." that very old cliché still says it well. Show how it is done, do it together, and then turn the work over to someone else.

A pastor should thank leaders regularly. Have some kind of training at least quarterly. Keep in touch monthly but allow the people in the class to carry out the ministries of the class.

Every leader has different management styles and skills. There may be different ways to the same conclusions and products. But clearly Ephesians 4:11-16 pushes the ministry down to the people of the church. To the parts of the body. Everyone is doing his part, in that paragraph. ABFs are a wonderful way to push that ministry to many different people!

But then they must be allowed to minister, to serve, to really reach out to others with their love!

The Church Has Too Few ABFs or Congregations

Many churches like this concept and get two Adult Bible Fellowships or perhaps three, and stop. Choices are important, and too few ABFs negates that.

I cannot write a chart on how many ABFs a church should have, but I would think that for every 50 adults in worship services within a month, there should be at least one ABF. And that if there are less than 150 adults who would be connected with a church there should be at least three or four ABFs anyway, so there can be a choice.

I would rather see a small church have three ABFs with only 15 in each rather than one main ABF, therefore having one main congregation which everyone must choose—whether it's the congregation as it meets in study or the congregation as it meets in worship.

We need choices.

We Think Big Is Better

That is just not true. If people want anything today or expect anything it is excellence. It is not enough just to have a growing church or to have numbers or to have many ABFs.

The goal for the church must be excellence and caring relationships. It must be good teaching in a setting where people know each other and are growing together so they can really know the Word.

The Church Often Expects Too Much Time

Older leaders of the church know that people used to give a lot more time to the church than they do now. Even people who are toward retirement age now back off sometimes, feeling burned out or like they have already done their share.

If once you could expect a volunteer to give six or eight hours a week, I think it's more like two or three these days. I'm talking about ministry after worship services.

And even the attendance at worship services is limited by people's philosophy now. Where once you could expect a very active person to come Sunday morning and Sunday evening and Wednesday evening, that certainly is not true now. Many of the strongest people come only Sunday morning for worship and perhaps to one other ministry or support group.

Therefore ABFs must be careful not to schedule so heavily that they simply push themselves out of the market for people in the church.

The Time Issue

There was a day when you could expect a very active church person to give 8 to 12 hours a week.

In those days many wives did not work and would volunteer a good segment of certain days for church ministries during the day, especially after their children were in school.

Now a large majority of mothers work, and schedules have families and singles moving so quickly. Leadership of a church must evaluate how many meetings or ministries can be expected, and prioritize what will be both sponsored and promoted.

We Act As If Teaching the Bible Is Enough

It is not. Maybe it should be. Maybe not.

Even Jesus did not just get up and teach. He formed relationships and got leaders involved.

People today seek application. They want to see how the Bible relates to life and what to do with it, and they want to hear from others.

The ABF structure is such that there should be a lot of that kind of teaching.

Perhaps Murphy's Law should be added as a final reason!

Actually, I have seen the ABF concept work well in many

different sizes of churches, and in churches of various moods. Pastors or other leaders have seen it help growth in small village churches or in large "mega-churches" in cities.

Work and pray to avoid the problems in this chapter, and you will have thriving Adult Bible Fellowships for the pleasure of God! And the good of the church.

NINE

Common Questions About ABFs

There are always common questions that come up when I talk about Adult Bible Fellowships. Here are some answers.

How do you know it works?
Our church first organized around the ABF concept in the early 1970s. That was in Ashland, Ohio when I had become so frustrated with all my lists of people and all the networking that seemed unmanageable.

I decided to put all the lists in one basket and structure the church around these "congregations" within the church. Aided by associate pastor John Teevan, who taught one of the three or four best ABFs I have ever seen, we put together this caring unit.

We wanted it to sound like an adult venture and to major on the Bible and fellowship—thus the name.

I have seen hundreds of small churches shift to this concept—it's not that big a shift of course. But it is different from the regular adult Sunday School.

It has worked extremely well in the larger church called The Chapel where I came in 1983. There were approximately 400 adults in the Sunday School then, and nine times that many in the worship services every Sunday—adults alone. The ABF concept has helped many people feel a part of The Chapel, promoted even more teaching, and quadrupled the involvement of adults so far in seven years.

What does this do with regular adult curriculum?
It simply means more adult curriculum material is used. And that's because adult classes grow.

The beauty of ABFs is that they can study whatever they choose. My opinion is that each adult class, with guidance from the pastor related to overall balance, should decide what it wants to study. This would be done by the leadership group, which includes the advisor/pastor, the teacher, the class leader, and the care leader. Sometimes the outreach leader is included as a member of this management team.

Young marrieds usually need one quarter or several months a year on marriage itself. I would hope that those in middle age would study something related to the adapting that comes in the 40s but only one or two months a year.

We ask all of our classes to study stewardship at least three or four Sundays a year. And we ask all of them to study missions once a year when we have that emphasis, and then usually the lessons are written from the office.

The rest of the time ABFs choose their own curriculum. All of the publishers have outstanding quarterlies and topics that can be used. Short books are wonderful for Adult Bible Fellowships, and many of the people will buy the books and use them for discussions.

How long should the topics be?
Most publishers use the 13-week mode. That's fine. But I think it is healthy to take five weeks on a certain subject now and then. You can pick the best chapters in a small book or simply discuss one main verse or chapter. Sometimes 13 weeks is too long to study Hebrews in a class like this.

The beauty of this system is that there is total flexibility. If after 13 weeks you want to continue in that same book for three more weeks, why not? Nobody is sitting there thinking, "It's March and it's time to change!" or "We always shifted at this time of the year when we were using the uniform lesson plans!"

The issue is interest and application and life-changes, and sometimes five weeks is plenty on a particular subject, and sometimes three or four months is better!

Again, the management team is such a help here. It isn't just one person deciding about curriculum; it's a team of people who are involved and understand the feelings of others in the class. They know their ABF because it's their ABF!

Of course we urge groups to have a good balance between Old and New Testament and to have purely practical how-to lessons thrown in occasionally.

A husband and wife team in our church at The Chapel go around and teach a three-week series on evangelism that has been well received. It emphasizes building bridges to unbelievers. It's a nice break for the regular teachers and great motivation for the class members, yet the ABF continues in its social ways and fellowship emphasis during this series also.

I have always encouraged classes to take a Sunday out now and then to study a special emphasis that the whole church is going through. I have forever been frustrated with studying Hebrews in Sunday School class, Psalms in the morning sermon, and the book of Acts in the evening sermon.

Should ABFs be under the regular Sunday School and church arrangement?

No.

The "regular" arrangement usually includes a church organizational chart set beside a Sunday School chart.

I remember one Sunday School superintendent saying to his pastor, "You take care of church, and I will take care of the Sunday School."

That's a fail-philosophy, but it is still enforced in many churches.

A better way is to see the Sunday School as very much a part of the church ministry, under the shepherding of the pastor and others who work with him to lead. Adult Bible Fellowships become part of the adult section of the education program or ministry.

Normally the pastor, someone else on staff, or an active layperson becomes the adult coordinator, often serving as the "adult pastoral advisor" for the Adult Bible Fellowships.

Then there is a youth director or youth pastor who cares for the whole youth area of the church, including the youth Sunday School. (In our church we call these classes YBFs — Youth Bible Fellowships.)

Then there is a children's coordinator or leader for the whole children's area of the ministry. This includes children's Sunday School, of course.

This horizontal arrangement seems much better than the whole vertical arrangement still present in many churches. Many churches have separate Sunday School constitutions, even treasuries. To them these are parallel corporations working side by side but not exactly mixing.

It was not too many years ago that one church growth institute came out with a kit that had directions for starting a breakthrough ministry in the church for evangelism and caring. It turned out to be the Adult Sunday School.

Once Sunday School was pure evangelism and the outreach of the church in the community. It still can be the best outreach arm of the church, especially when its adult groups are formed into Adult Bible Fellowships that have outreach strategy and caring ministry.

All of this is best accomplished when it is part of the major strategy of the church, under united leadership.

Should a church simply shift to this whole ministry style quickly?

Not overnight. Slow transition is necessary for almost any major change in a church. (Every change involves movement and all movement produces friction and friction includes pain.)

The best approach is to begin one Adult Bible Fellowship

using the caring and social and fellowship organizational chart, and working with three leaders and a pastoral advisor to really give it strength and direction.

As people become a part of the ABF and it really functions to meet their needs and provide fellowship and a study environment, the word will get around the church. Other classes will want their structure to be similar.

Success breeds success, and other classes can be moved toward this same style.

The worst thing would be to go in to your church announcing a major sweep in change, alarming people, and sending off negative or defensive reactions. Or maybe an earthquake.

Changes toward ABFs are really not that major physically. Most churches are already adaptable in this area, but most need the new structure and the change.

How important is it that ABFs be by age groupings?

I think it is very important. All of us tend to have our best friends among those who are our own age, or close, or have children the age of our children.

That's the way ABFs are organized.

I encourage larger churches to have some ABFs that are not linked to age. These could be electives or simply classes built around a certain approach or a certain teacher. But for the most part, strong fellowship and ministry ties will be with people of similar age.

Usually it is the older people in the church who do not like that. They sometimes feel segregated. "Why are you shoving us off to the side?" one asked me when we were moving toward ABFs.

That cerainly is not the intent. Older couples can be used to start the younger classes. They can be used as teachers, or models, and many socials or projects bring together two or three classes or different age groups. Home Bible classes and other fellowships can include a large age span.

But the best ABFs are going to involve people of similar age span. Think who your best friends are. Most of them are close to you in age. That's just the way we relate.

What if the elective system is working well and we would choose to stay with it?
Fine. Simply count the cost of not organizing so that long-term relationships are gained. Be sure that this is available in another part of the church.

And, what are the other main ways that fellowship and caring can be organized in a church?

Many churches have used the neighborhood concept, or at least tried to use it. Many churches have tried the "zip code" system, but it is frustrating because people cross several zip codes to get to the church they like, and often to get to the friends they want. Most of us would not necessarily call a neighbor at a time of need, but probably a friend across town.

That's why I believe the ABF concept is better—it makes use of some natural affinities to help produce the very Biblical fellowship affinity.

Many churches are organized around a cell relationship, where home Bible studies become the caring system. This can work very well. Prominent in Korea, that does not mean this method will be a success wherever it is tried. Many people are afraid of the smaller cells, and these do not provide the same span of fellowship or mix of age groups and varieties.

I personally believe that a larger group is more of the New Testament challenge. The mix of different backgrounds and opinions and problems can be very healthy when there are 40-60-80 people. This causes many different chemistries to flow, and out of the tensions and the challenge come Christian growth as well as more love ministries to each other.

Why not just the good old fashioned name, Sunday School class?
That's fine for some. Our experience in church has shown that many see Sunday School as being for children, so the new name at least makes a point about the target.

The new name also emphasizes the book we study (The Bible!) and the fellowship issues that are so vital. We retain the title Sunday School for our children's classes, and have YBFs (Youth Bible Fellowships).

Should there be separate classes for singles?
Yes and no.

Yes, singles would like to study certain subjects and to have fellowships on their own, but they certainly should not be barred from the other classes. The best way is to have one or two or three main singles classes, but then encourage them to join any of the other classes. Some may prefer to try a regular couples' class.

Unless the class is strictly for couples and going to study marriage most of the time, I encourage classes not to name themselves "Young Marrieds" or "Life Couples" or a title that calls for just couples.

Titles can be embarrassing when analyzed carefully. Many churches have used "Pairs 'n' Spares," which hardly would be a complimentary title for a single!

How do you keep the age grouping? Do people go to a new class every five years?
The ages listed for classes are general—perhaps "late 30s" or "Parents of Teens" or "Forties" would be the label. Then the age descriptions simply keep changing as the class gets older.

I have never yet met a 40-year-old who came up to me the Sunday after his fortieth birthday, saluted, and said, "Sir, I was 40 this week and I'll be reporting to a new class." People like to stay with the people they are just getting to know.

When ABFs really work, the tie is close and people do not want to leave. In addition, this kind of work for fellowship is hard enough that it takes time. It is not settled in one year or one week.

What if you are one of the church education leaders or just very active in an adult class and you want to do this but your pastor does not want to?
Then don't do it.

What is the best process of trying to change someone's mind if he does not want to change?
Change comes hard. If you are one of the members of an adult class and your teacher or other leaders do not want to switch to this format, perhaps you should just give up or just pray—not that the two are the same.

Perhaps this book would help. Perhaps a visit to another church or correspondence or a phone call with someone in a class where it is working this way would explain that the differences are not so negative at all but can breed such positive results.

But go slowly. When people feel like you are rushing them to change their mind, they make their mind stronger the other way.

Can this system be combined with electives?
Yes. The church can have the best of both worlds—the fellowships and caring systems and organization of an ABF as well as the variety of electives.

We try to keep electives to four or five weeks usually, allowing people who shift from their regular ABF to take a special subject but still come back to their social and fellowship connections.

I think it captures the best of both worlds.

In three or four areas we have special training programs that we hope everyone in the church goes through, and so these are offered frequently during the year and repeated so that new people can take them.

Here are some of the subjects:

1. Pastor's Membership Class.

This is a ten-session course that provides orientation about the church's doctrines and practices, as well as ten minutes of commercials each class for various ministries in the church. This is required for membership but also gives people a review of basic doctrines and the church and what it believes.

2. Bible Basics.

One of our lay couples teaches a ten-week course on how to study the Bible, what we believe, basic thoughts about evangelism or apologetics. We encourage all new Christians to take this as well as new members who have not had a lot of Bible training.

3. Parents of Teens.

We have a special course for parents of adolescents or preadolescents, preparing them for this great time of life. This elective happens to run for about 18 weeks for each subject, 36 for the year, it's such an important subject that it's healthy to do it this way, though some of the ABF involvement suffers as people stay out so long.

4. Learning to Pray.

A four-week elective on prayer can be a very stimulating one, especially because many people do not pray. We take too much for granted in this area.

5. How to Study the Bible.

Here's another special subject that can be taught in the regular ABF, but people are in such various stages of Bible study. This course is designed as a survey of the Bible, and it is also an excellent one for new people.

6. Newcomers' Orientation.

This one is a little different and is really meant for people brand-new to the church who do not know what an ABF is or who are not plugged into one. For three weeks they are asked to meet in this orientation to get to know the church. The class includes a tour of the church building, a presentation of ABFs and other ministries, and a look at various other facets of the church.

We do not teach a lot. We simply try to emphasize what we believe about the Bible and what we believe about salvation, making those important issues clear.

We began this when we realized that the first class many people took was the Pastor's Membership Class, which is quite a commitment to make very early in your attendance at a church. From the beginning, Newcomers Orientation has had a good response. After the third week we close with a 40 minute reception on Sunday evening before the evening service, when pastors come in and simply meet the people. I go to make a presentation of church philosophy and answer questions and meet them.

7. *Child Dedication.*

Before parents dedicate their children in the services, they spend two or three weeks together with each other to talk about what it means to raise children in the ways of Christ. They also study what the vows mean that they will make publicly and gather ideas and books and stimulation on the Christian home.

8. *Current Topics.*

During the Iraq war or right afterward we ran a three-week elective on what the Bible says about the Middle East and Babylon.

Isn't is dangerous to put pastoral care and social life and fellowship and so many essentials of a local church into one part of that church, into one class structure? Or even to call that class a "congregation" of the church?

An ABF may be dangerous, in the sense that something very good might happen! It might also be dangerous, in the sense that a class could get so self-reliant that it detaches from the church in other areas. I have not had that happen except in a few cases when it would have happened no matter how the class was structured.

I would think it's always true that if a class tried to detach from the church, there are other problems anyway, and the problems are not in structure or the ABF system.

Any perceived danger must be weighed against the obvious good of course.

I would say it is dangerous to pretend that classes are meeting needs they are not. And it is dangerous to have so many differ-

94

ent structures and forms for fellowship or caring in a church that they cannot be managed or coordinated.

It is dangerous to urge the people to fulfill the "one another" commands as given in Scripture but then not provide the means for them to do that for or to each other.

It is dangerous to urge fellowship when it is hard to find it; dangerous to tell people they ought to be getting to know each other when they never meet together in smaller groups; dangerous to expect discipleship if there is no structure for it.

Perhaps *dangerous* is too strong a word for all that, but I do want to point out the trade-offs.

You mention that 20 or 30 to 70 or 80 is the best size for an ABF. Do you always split them when they get bigger than that?

I almost always wish we would have! Because 80 or 90 at the extreme is the largest group where people can know each other and really do some functioning as a "community" or "congregation," ABFs should divide when they consistently run 60 or 70 or 80. Where I have allowed exceptions for that in our own church, the classes usually level off at about 80 or 90 anyway, and then it is harder to divide to grow later because people get so used to their own class.

The best way is to keep starting new classes, often using a few "pioneers" from an ABF to start the new one. It can be very difficult to get people to split a class with good chemistry.

What are some essentials to remember when dividing?

Don't force it. Don't tell people what class to go to. Go with a challenge, "We hope 40 percent will go and 40 percent will stay," and then work behind the scenes to get a leadership team for the new class. That leadership team then recruits pioneers who will help start the class so that by the time it is ready to start and is announced many times, 20-25 percent of the existing ABF have agreed to start a new class.

I use "40 percent go and 40 percent stay" with tongue in cheek and a smile so people know we are not demanding that anyone do anything!

If 40 percent go or even 30 percent, everyone wins!

Sometimes if a very popular teacher has helped build the class, we urge that teacher to teach both sections for awhile to show that one is not varsity and the other junior varsity.

Can youth classes function like ABF?

Many of the same purposes can be carried out. It might be harder to have the care unit leaders function in the same way, though kids usually rise to do what they're asked to do.

If you had a church of about 80 or 90 regular adults who were all in one class, and they loved it there, and that was the only adult Sunday School class, how would you begin to incorporate the principles of this ABF concept?

Carefully but quickly!

The goal might be to have at least four ABFs with these same people, and grow from there.

I would start with a special subject for the young marrieds, an obvious one for them with an elective-type class that would last six or ten weeks. If that functioned well, and I assume it would, the class could grow into a regular class.

The goal with that many people would be to have one for young marrieds, one for middles, one for older, and an elective that could meet special needs.

Wouldn't involvement in an ABF keep people from doing other things in the church?

This is a valid criticism, and the only weakness that I have found in the ABF system. Sometimes people get so involved in the caring ministry of their own class that they may drop out of other ministries in the church.

The good side is that they're helping meet real needs of people, not just doing busy work. They are ministering to their peers, or helping with outreach in their ABF.

But the bad side is that it can affect other ministries in that church.

One goal is to simply urge people to have one main ministry, and to protect the other ministries by emphasizing the needs of those ministries also and helping people choose where their gifts and concerns can best be used. But then there must be a sense of being willing to simply relax about what people choose also. They should serve where they really want to.

APPENDIX A

Job Descriptions

ABF Pastor

I. **GOALS:**
To give pastoral direction, advice and care to an Adult Bible Fellowship, making sure that it is organized and functioning according to our ideals and goals for an ABF.

II. **RESPONSIBLE TO:**
Senior and Associate Pastors, in general policy areas; Minister of Adult Education as the leader of ABFs in terms of actual organization and ABF functions; Minister of Pastoral Care for the area of Pastoral Care.

III. **ABF PASTOR'S RESPONSIBILITIES:**
A. Supervise organization of ABF so that there is strong teaching, a class leader and appropriate support group, and a care organization. Help these leaders carry out their ministries. Be reponsible for their accountability.
B. Be responsible for pastoral care for people in that ABF.
C. Be responsible for initiating evangelism and outreach opportunities toward people who want to be in the ABF or assigned to that care system.
D. Be sure that the ABF functions in line with all church policies, goals, schedules, and unity. Be the liaison of communication with all the main leaders — sharing church needs, mood, and challenges.
E. Train and meet with the main leaders of the ABF — Teacher, ABF Leader, and Care Leaders. (Please present all names for potential ABF leadership positions in our Pastoral Staff Meetings for confirmation approval.)
F. Train, supervise, and help the Care Coordinator with the care leaders of the ABFs, the under shepherds who help care for people.
G. Be available as a pastor to those in the ABF who call on

you and also seek to give shepherding care to all who come under the care of that ABF. Be sure their needs are met. Take initiative when there is a need.

H. Report regularly to the Minister of Adult Education about the progress of the ABF in terms of growth, mood, and goals.

I. Be sure that each class has monthly (or an appropriate number) of ABF socials. Attend classes and socials whenever possible. Seek to be close to the people in the ABF.

J. Be responsible for getting publicity out about ABF activities.

K. Please be praying daily for your ABF(s) and for the leadership, by name. You must get these people in your heart.

ABF Leader

I. GOALS:
To help generate and maintain fellowship within the ABF, to start the class on time, and to maintain the class schedule.

II. REQUIREMENTS:
A. Be an active, growing Christian.
B. Be a member or in the process of becoming a member of The Chapel.
C. Be active in the ABF class.
D. Willing to subscribe to The Chapel's "Spiritual Qualifications for Leadership" statement.
E. Willing to fulfill the ministry description.
F. Regular Sunday service attendance.

III. APPOINTMENT:
By ABF Class Teacher with approval of Pastoral Advisor.

IV. RESPONSIBLE TO:
ABF Class Teacher and ABF Pastoral Advisor.

V. TERM OF MINISTRY:
One year:_____ to _____.

VI. ABF CLASS LEADER'S RESPONSIBILITIES:
A. Set overall mood and direction of the ABF.
B. Help people relax: encourage participation in coffee and fellowship time.
C. Know how to start the class promptly and give teacher sufficient time for lesson.
D. Arrange for periodic testimonies. Ask someone to share briefly about his or her life so it sets the pace for warmth, fellowship, and more caring.
E. Vary the set-up of the room in communication with the

teacher to provide a variety of atmospheres and arrangements.

F. Maintain proper communication with teacher, pastoral advisor, and other class officers.

G. Participate in the scheduled ABF teachers' and leaders' meetings as called, usually the third Sunday at 5:00 p.m.

H. Know the goals of the church and how ABFs relate to Sunday morning.

I. Maintain a current class roster.

ABF Care Captain

I. GOALS
To encourage the people to become active in Christ and His church; to build relationships and participate in the small care groups.

II. REQUIREMENTS
A. Be an active, growing Christian.
B. Be a member or in the process of becoming a member of The Chapel.
C. Be active in the ABF class.
D. Willing to subscribe to The Chapel's "Spiritual Qualifications for Leadership" statement.
E. Willing to fulfill the ministry description.
F. Regular Sunday service attendance.

III. APPOINTMENT:
By ABF Teacher with approval of Pastor Advisor and Class Leader.

IV. RESPONSIBLE TO:
The ABF Class Teacher and Leader.

V. TERM OF MINISTRY:
One year:_____ to _____.

VI. RESPONSIBILITIES:
A. Select sufficient number of care group leaders with approval of class teacher and leader.
B. Divide the class membership into groups of not more than 10 households per group.
C. Call regular care group leaders' meetings (suggest quarterly) for information, instruction, and inspiration.

D. Participate in care group training sessions as scheduled by The Chapel's Care Pastor; encourage group leaders to participate also.
E. Through the care leaders keep entire class informed of special needs such as illness, loss of loved one, etc.
F. Maintain prayer communication with other class officers and the teacher.
G. Know the goals of the church and how ABFs relate to Sunday morning.

ABF Prayer Leader

I. GOALS:
To develop, foster, and maintain a spirit of prayer and worship at all class activities; to lead the class in a weekly prayer time emphasis.

II. REQUIREMENTS:
A. Be an active, growing Christian.
B. Be a member or in the process of becoming a member of The Chapel.
C. Be active in the ABF class.
D. Willing to subscribe to The Chapel's "Spiritual Qualifications for Leadership" statement.
E. Willing to fulfill the ministry description.
F. Regular Sunday service attendance.

III. APPOINTMENT:
By ABF Teacher with approval of Pastor Advisor and Class Leader.

IV. RESPONSIBLE TO:
The ABF Class Teacher and Leader.

V. TERM OF MINISTRY:
One year:_____ to _____.

VI. RESPONSIBILITIES:
A. Maintain a spirit of prayer in the class.
B. Lead the class in prayer emphasis each week.
C. Keep before the class regularly the prayer needs of members.
D. Receive from care captains the class's special prayer requests and needs.

E. Develop prayer projects for the class as a unit.
F. Maintain prayer communication with other class officers and the teachers.
G. Know the goals of the church and how ABFs relate to Sunday morning.

ABF Host

I. GOALS:
To help the people who visit the class to feel at home and comfortable and to create an atmosphere of "glad you came and come back regularly.

II. REQUIREMENTS:
A. Be an active, growing Christian.
B. Be a member or in the process of becoming a member of The Chapel.
C. Be active in the ABF class.
D. Willing to subscribe to The Chapel's "Spiritual Qualifications for Leadership" statement.
E. Willing to fulfill the ministry description.
F. Regular Sunday service attendance.

III. APPOINTMENT:
By ABF Teacher with approval of Pastoral Advisor and Class Leader.

IV. RESPONSIBLE TO:
Class Leader and Teacher.

V. TERM OF MINISTRY:
One year:_____ to _____.

VI. RESPONSIBILITIES:
A. Welcome regular members each week.
B. Greet guests, register them, and introduce them to several members of the class.
C. Give registration to teacher for follow-up letter.
D. Host the guests in worship if attending after class; be sure they can get around the building and find their way.

E. Arrange for someone to greet and host in your place if absent.

F. Maintain proper communication with the teacher and class officers.

G. Know the goals of the church and how ABFs relate to Sunday morning.

Special Events and Projects Leader

I. GOALS:
To organize and execute three or four special activities, involving as many class members as possible.

II. REQUIREMENTS:
A. Be an active, growing Christian.
B. Be a member or in the process of becoming a member of The Chapel.
C. Be active in the ABF class.
D. Willing to subscribe to The Chapel's "Spiritual Qualifications for Leadership" statement.
E. Willing to fulfill the ministry description.
F. Regular Sunday service attendance.

III. APPOINTMENT:
By Class Teacher with approval of Class Leader.

IV. RESPONSIBLE TO:
Class Teacher and Leader.

V. TERM OF MINISTRY:
One year:_____ to _____.

VI. RESPONSIBILITIES:
A. Create, plan, promote, and carry out three or four special projects or events each year.
B. Provide sufficient information, instructions, and inspiration in order that the class members will "want to" participate.
C. Work closely with the teacher and other officers in the preparation of the activities.
D. Maintain proper communication with teacher and other class officers.
E. Know the goals of the church and how ABFs relate to Sunday morning.

ABF Social Leader

I. **GOALS:**
To help generate fellowship within the ABF and coordinate and plan class socials.

II. **REQUIREMENTS:**
A. Be an active, growing Christian.
B. Be a member or in the process of becoming a member of The Chapel.
C. Be active in the ABF class.
D. Willing to subscribe to The Chapel's "Spiritual Qualifications for Leadership" statement.
E. Willing to fulfill the ministry description.
F. Regular Sunday service attendance.

III. **APPOINTMENT:**
By Class Teacher with approval of Class Leader.

IV. **RESPONSIBLE TO:**
Class Teacher and Leader.

V. **TERM OF MINISTRY:**
One year:_____ to _____.

VI. **RESPONSIBILITIES:**
A. Arrange for the provision of refreshments for ABF class each week.
B. Plan sufficient social opportunities and parties during the year to get maximum fellowship and love.
C. Maintain proper communication with the teacher and other class officers.

ABF Teacher

I. GOALS:
To lead the ABF in learning through dynamic Bible teaching and to set the overall mood and direction of the ABF for biblical instruction.

II. REQUIREMENTS:
- A. Be an active, growing Christian.
- B. Be a member of The Chapel.
- C. Be active in the ABF class.
- D. Willing to subscribe to The Chapel's "Spiritual Qualification for Leadership" statement.
- E. Willing to fulfill the ministry description.
- F. Regular Sunday service attendance.

III. APPOINTMENT:
By pastoral staff.

IV. RESPONSIBLE TO:
The ABF Pastor and Minister of Adult Education.

V. ABF TEACHER RESPONSIBILITIES:
- A. The teacher leads by example as well as by instruction. Therefore, the teacher must be giving evidences of the fruit of the Spirit as outlined in Galatians 5:22-23.
- B. The teacher must be doctrinally sound. He should be in complete agreement with the articles of faith as outlined in the doctrinal position of The Chapel. No teacher should privately or publicly teach anything adverse to the doctrinal position of The Chapel.
- C. The teacher should be faithful to the public services of the church. Those in places of leadership should set the example for those who follow. This should include at least the

110

following: the attendance in an ABF; in the morning worship hour; and in the Wednesday evening services. People
are always encouraged when they find their teacher in attendance with them in the church's services.

D. The teacher should be faithful and prompt in arrival to the
class.

E. The teacher should be loyal to the pastor and to the church
program. The teacher should be willing to cooperate with
the desire of those in the church's leadership and be loyal to
the pastor as he presents the church's program under the
direction of God.

F. The teacher should attend announced ABF faculty meetings. The teacher's attendance in these meetings is a part of
his or her necessary teaching preparation.

G. The teacher should contact the Minister of Adult Education or his or her ABF Pastor by Wednesday night or as
soon as possible if he is unable to teach his ABF on Sunday.
It is recognized that family and health emergencies arise and
these emergencies are lovingly understood in Christian
kindness.

APPENDIX B

What the Church of the Future Will Look Like

As I write this I am finishing my 25th year of pastoral ministry. So much has changed and we've only just begun!

People who like to divide the history timetables into decades and use decimal points tell us that the ten years of the 90s will bring more change than the 30 years before! And that's quite a bit. While the 80s left us morally exhausted, the beginning of the 90s showed us that change was going to take off like space shuttles, but not necessarily toward the heavens!

Times Have Changed

There are few traditions anymore. Nobody drives a Ford because his grandfather did, or knows his banker very personally, and most of these huge changes will affect the church.

- *Mobility.* People not only move from city to city more easily than before, but also from church to church. Many middle-aged or young adults claim two or three churches, rather than one, as their home church(es).

- *Coloring.* By the end of this millennium, white Anglo-Saxon protestants in most big cities will be the minority rather than the moral majority.

- *Graying.* People are getting older, and there's a larger group of seniors than ever before. Ministries to seniors will be affected in every size church.

- *Pluralism.* This philosophy—that you can have one belief but accept every other belief as being equally valid—is rampant, even in the church. We live in a pluralistic society, and the church is already affected.

- *Short commitments.* We blame this trend on baby boomers, but it's happening everywhere. People might commit to a ten-week discipleship course, but not to a three-month 2:7 course. People might say they'll try something out for a short time, but they want to know how long they are obligated. Short commitments show up in marriages, divorces, and in many areas of ethical values.

● Cocooning. This term describes ordering a pizza with your car phone on the way home from work and then picking up a video so you can stay home on Friday evening with your wife or family.

● *Consumerism.* People are leaving the church because they aren't getting anything out of it, and that's their main reason for church attendance.

● *Fun and Experience.* These are the watchwords of the generation that lives for self and stuff.

Many people live as if right now is forever, and it is not. There is so much more.

Most younger adults assert that they want to have certain needs met:

1. To be loved;
2. To make a difference;
3. To have security;
4. To have comfort.

I know a place where at least three of these needs can be met pretty readily. I know a church. But we must keep up with the changes or stay ahead of them without changing our theology or our beliefs.

In addition to all these changes happening right now, I look back on 25 years of pastoring and see so many more:

● *Attention span.* It's much shorter than before. (I won't elaborate anymore right now because you probably want to read another point.)

● *Family.* So many children had two parents then. Now we talk constantly of the dysfunctional family.

● *Expectations.* Church people today have fewer expectations of the pastor, but these expectations are much different now. (I'll elaborate on these more in the list ahead.)

● *Working women.* Everybody has to bring this issue up, but it's very noticeable. Women (and men) have fewer volunteer hours available.

● *Catholicism.* Twenty-five years ago it was protestants, or at least some of them, who attacked the Pope. Now it is Catholics.

● *Television.* What a difference this friend and foe has made. It has so influenced the values and the passivity of families and individuals. We were so shocked when we saw J.F. Kennedy get shot one day, but now nothing would shock us on TV.

● *Seekers.* So many are more openly talking about their need for faith or their desire to know more. This can be very healthy for the church.

● *Sunday evening service.* It's dying in many churches.

• *Morality.* It died in many homes. In 1968 *The New York Times* carried twelve articles in a row about a female at Boston University who was living with a male (not her husband) off campus. It was that different.

Reaching Our Culture
The ethical questions of today and of the years ahead are hardly whether a church should have a unified budget! Christ will build His church. His church will survive.

But unless we seek to reach the culture and people to whom we have been assigned, we are not "going into all the world" in the way Christ commanded.

We depend on Him. Above all we must sense His grace, proclaim the Gospel, and live in obedient trust.

The following methods added to this dependence can help bring effective strength to the church. Based on studies of the future, books about tomorrow and developing trends, here are suggestions for ways the church can stay current and be strong in the next years:

1. Authority with Love
The church must speak with Schwartzkopfien answers more than with press secretarial answers. Telling the truth, but with love.

The time for the church to have its set of no-answer answers is gone. People want to hear truth. Even some unbelievers have often expressed their desires to see the church saying more or saying it clearly.

Committee-created beliefs or George Gallup Poll opinions have designed the statement of faith for some who do not know what to say when they wish to say what they believe, but they are sure they don't want to go against the stream.

Only the church can really help.

Few argue with the hardly prophetic statement that it's getting worse than ever before, but few want to talk about how to alter the raging river.

The church must speak with authority, but also with love.

Many churches have spoken with just one or the other. No question about that. I personally do not think that either church will be strong in the next ten years.

"Truthing it in love" is a way of life, but it is also a way of preaching and teaching for a church, and clearly biblical.

If we do not do it this way, I think the world will turn somewhere else. Even people outside the church expect the church to give clear answers — truth that is revealed. People looking for hope in their lives do not want someone who says "aw shucks" about God or morality.

The church that will be strong will speak with authority. But not provide answers that thump the Bible or hit people on the head without grace.

Naturally, I am prejudiced because of my belief in inspiration of Scriptures, but I believe that churches that speak with authority and remain with the Word of God will have a much better chance of growth. (I'm speaking in human terms and marketing terms.) I also believe that's what God wants us to do.

But I stress again, "with love!"

2. Reality with Application
"God talk" will wear out even more in the future. I mean using a language at church that most people do not understand.

People will be even less interested in what happened in Ephesus or Asia Minor unless they understand that it is God's Word written from there or about there but applied to the reality of today's world. That must be stressed.

Because of where people are and where they will be in the next ten or fifteen years, I believe that they will attend churches where their real lives are addressed.

I have never had anyone come up to me and ask me to recite some of the things I memorized in seminary, but I have had them look me in the eye and ask about marriage or what the meaning of life is or where they should go next.

The Bible is certainly real and profitable for our lives, wherever we live. But we must stress this and be able to teach it and help people apply to their lives.

Feedback from people in classes will be even more important.

Churches will need to address difficult ethical questions: medical and health issues, changes in methods of how the church operates, the role of women, sexuality and righteousness, war and death, as well as other very personal questions and decisions.

3. Worship with Involvement
A wonderful wave has already swept through many churches and brought healthy renewal of worship. People participate. They do not want to just "watch others worship," as one young adult explained special music to me. They want to be involved, to have a strong part.

115

Some things help make this happen:

● Worship choruses that bridge generations, with involvement, and real words that communicate what the singers really feel.

● "Accumulation" of worship and worship music—planning events in sequence so the mood of worship develops and is not so interrupted by the "non-worship" segments such as announcements and missions moments.

● More emphasis on worshiping in personal life so that people are better at corporate worship.

● Less emphasis on "special music" and more on all the people singing to God.

● Instruction on how to participate in the service rather than assuming everyone already knows how.

4. Commitment with Diversity
The church must call for a strong allegiance to Christ. He Himself did. The healthy church in the future will not dilute its message or doctrine to be culturally relevant. The call instead is to be scripturally accurate.

But the needs of people and the trends among believers call for a better emphasis on Christian liberty. There must be more flexibility on minor issues.

● Leaders must work hard, showing strong commitment, modeling what faith and a ministry heart really produce.

● Teaching must emphasize commitment and obedience, not a "lite" Christianity.

● Allowance must be made for divergent views.

● Publicity must begin for a large mission—to win the world.

5. "High Touch" with Community
The church must meet the needs of an age of high technology but low touchology! And there are many ways the church can be really good at this.

● Provide "congregation life" within the church, so that people have groups they can get into where they will know each other and grow together. Any church over 70 or 80 adults must have choices in these areas. (This is the ABF system.)

● Foster openness within each of these communities and groups, which allows people to share real love and growth together.

● Maintain a pulpit that is transparent—not a glass lectern but a person who leads with openness and a willingness to share his struggles as well as his successes!

• Provide target groups that meet real needs for specific groups of people: a club for young mothers where they study small children and their special needs; small groups for men where it is not a sin to have failures or to struggle as a man but where you learn how to love a woman and lead a family.

6. Speciality Groups with Support

The church that keeps growing in a healthy way will have a number of groups within the church to give special, specific support. All of us wonder if these needs were around before and unlabeled or if the pressures of today's world have produced them?

• Groups for single parents, with support on how to face the challenges.

• Groups for people considering full-time ministries, a "Fellowship of the Yoke" to help them get ready and sharpen each other.

• A group for a number of special dysfunctions—adult children of alcoholics, people who grapple with eating disorders, etc. People can grapple with these in the context of Christ and His strength and in personal relationships that can be trusted and can be so very edifying. The church is a good place to have this kind of special support.

• Wives of unbelieving husbands.

• CEOs or managers, people who feel the pressures of leading others.

• Groups within the various age groups.

7. Excellence with Integrity

It may be because baby boomers demand it or because the culture has seen enough shallowness, but excellence, with integrity, must characterize the healthy church of the years ahead. The growing, healthy church, at least.

Excellence may mean that the nurseries are painted and very clean, or that the restrooms are the same. Or it may mean any of the following:

• The services are planned well, usually with a theme, with a relationship between the ingredients of the service.

• Job descriptions exist and good volunteers are gathered for the various ministries of the church, from greeting to those who follow-up people who trust Christ.

• Excellence is obvious in the building. While it does not have to be perfectly designed, it can be clean and inviting.

● Excellence is obvious in programs for children and youth.

● Church governing procedures are simpler, with less red tape and wide boundaries for pastors to lead within budget and philosophy of ministry.

Integrity that has been so questioned and so violated in some churches and in the public religious sector must be guarded very carefully.

● Finances are handled with proper care and integrity.

● The books are audited rather than acting as if the church does not need such guardianship.

● The pastors and other church leaders exhibit personal and moral integrity. More churches will have a "minister's or leader's agreement" that everyone must sign and adhere to, not so much emphasizing specific social habits but personal integrity and obedience to Christ.

● No more false advertising, or promising the sky when the program is only ten feet high.

● Saying it clearly when the Bible says it clearly, but acknowledging when it is not clear in the Scriptures. Hopefully, people will do as the Bereans once did in the Book of Acts, and check the Bible rather than accepting someone's opinion as God's Word.

8. Specialization with Smorgasbord!

The outreach program of the church that is reaching new people these days and into the next century will not be tied to one main evangelism method or the regular missions program of the church. Instead, the church will continue to build side doors to provide more ways for people to come in:

● Support groups to help with various needs of people, much like the support groups within the church.

● Help for outsiders in marriage and family.

● Strong youth events and attention to problems of youth.

● Attention to the growing seniors area.

● Action love or special people needs such as for those in poverty.

● Sports and music ministries.

BIBLIOGRAPHY

Carrier, Wallace H. *Teaching Adults in Sunday School.* Nashville: Convention Press, 1976.

Coleman Jr., Lucien E. *Understanding Adults.* Nashville: Convention Press, 1969.

Jacobsen, Henry. *You Can Teach Adults.* Wheaton: Victor Books, 1983.

Loth, Paul E. *Tips for Teaching Adults.* Wheaton: Evangelical Teacher Training Association, 1978.

McBride, Neal. *Equipping Adults through Bible Study.* Glendale, Calif.: International Center for Learning, 1977.

_____, *The Adult Class: Caring for Each Other.* Glendale, Calif.: International Center for Learning, 1977.

Marlowe, Monroe & Bobbie Reed. *Creative Bible Learning.* Glendale, Calif.: International Center for Learning, 1971.

Murray, Dick. *Strengthening the Adult Sunday School Class.* Nashville: Abingdon, 1981.

Peterson, Gilbert A. *How to Get Results with Adults.* Wheaton: Victor Books, 1973.

Richards, Lawrence O. *You and Adults.* Chicago: Moody Press, 1974.

Robinson, Floyd. *Electives Working for You.* Wheaton: Victor Books, 1972.

Stewart, Ed. *Teaching Adults through Discussion.* Glendale, Calif.: International Center for Learning, 1978.

Wilbert, Warren N. *Teaching Christian Adults.* Grand Rapids: Baker Book House, 1980.

Zuck, Roy B. & Gene A. Getz. *Adult Education in the Church.* Chicago: Moody Press, 1970.